Death Valley Ghost Towns – As They Appear Today

Robert C. Jones

Robert Jones
P.O. Box 1775
Kennesaw, GA 30156

jone442@bellsouth.net
rcjbooks.com

"Death Valley Ghost Towns – As They Appear Today", Copyright 2010, 2013 by Robert C. Jones. All rights reserved.

Second Edition

ISBN: 1453788638
EAN-13: 9781453788639

This book is dedicated to my wife Debra, who has traveled many miles with me down poor mining roads in Death Valley and the Mojave.

Table of Contents

Table of Contents...4
Introduction..6
Death Valley – East Side...9
    Amargosa Borax Works..9
    Ashford Mine (Golden Treasure Mine)..11
    Bonnie Claire..13
    Bullfrog...15
    Carrara...17
    Chloride Cliff..19
    Death Valley Junction..21
    Gladstone Mine...23
    Greenwater District...26
    Ibex Springs..28
    Inyo Mines..30
    Kasson...33
    Keane Springs...36
    Keane Wonder Mine..38
    Leadfield..41
    Lee/Lee Annex...43
    Lila C. Mine ("Old Ryan")...46
    Longstreet Cabin...47
    Monarch Canyon Mine...49
    Rhodes Spring...51
    Rhyolite...53
    Ryan..57
    Salt Spring Hills (Amargosa Mines)..59
    Saratoga Springs...61
    Scotty's Castle...63
    Shoshone Caves..65
    Strozzi Ranch..69
    Tecopa Mines..71
Death Valley West Side...77

- Aguereberry Camp/Eureka Mine/Harrisburg..................................77
- Argenta Mine...79
- Ashford Mill..81
- Ballarat...83
- Barker Ranch..87
- Broken Pick/Trail Canyon...91
- Christmas Mine..94
- Corona Mine (Jail Canyon)...96
- Crater...99
- Darwin..102
- Eagle Borax Works/Shorty Harris Grave......................................105
- Galena Canyon...106
- Goldbelt..108
- Greene-Denner-Drake Mill..110
- Harmony Borax Works...112
- Hungry Bill's Ranch..115
- Journigan's Mill..118
- Keystone Mine (Lotus Mine)...120
- Lippincott Mine..122
- Lost Burro Mine...124
- Old Stovepipe Wells..125
- Owl Hole Springs/Black Magic & New Deal Mines.....................127
- Panamint City..128
- Queen of Sheba Mine/Carbonate...130
- Skidoo..132
- Starr's Mill..135
- Tucki Mountain..137
- Ubehebe Mine...139
- Warm Springs Camp/Gold Hill Mill...141
- Wildrose Canyon Kilns...144

Maps..145
Sources...153
About the Author...155

Introduction

> "I am unable to give all the required information. Have been in this mining district 3 years but never was at the County Seat. Am within 12 miles of the great Death Valley, and if I remain here much longer, will be nearer some other death valley." (Isaac G. Messic, in an 1877 application for a post office for Panamint City (National Archives))

1925 photo shows the hazards of travel in Death Valley (from the collection of Juanita Kasson Ingram)

Death Valley is truly an amazing place. It contains the lowest point in the Western Hemisphere (Badwater, -282 feet below sea level), but is surrounded by extremely tall mountain peaks (including Telescope Peak, at 11,049 feet above sea level!). The park itself contains 3,336,000 acres (90% wilderness), making it the largest national park in the contiguous United States.

Death Valley is also, of course, one of the driest and hottest spots in the world. Average rainfall per year is only 1.65 inches! The average high temperature in July is 116.2! (The highest temperature ever recorded there was 134 degrees).

Death Valley has a fascinating mining history. Miners first passed through here in 1849 during the California gold rush, not realizing that there were vast deposits of gold and borax just waiting to be taken out of the mountains and Valley floor. By the late 19th century though, large scale gold and borax mining operations were in full swing. In the 20th century, talc mining would join borax as the two most important minerals mined in the Death Valley area.

Ghost towns in general are fast decaying away, the victims of weather, vandals and shoddy construction. The 100+ ghost towns and mining camps within and near Death Valley are probably in better shape than most because of the preservative affect of the extremely dry climate, and the protection offered by Death Valley being a National Park (and, earlier, a National Monument). However, the ghost towns here are slowly fading away.

In some cases, whole towns (such as Harrisburg or Schwab) have disappeared so completely that it is almost as if they never existed. One should keep in mind, though, the temporary nature of many of these boom and bust mining towns. Harrisburg, for example, was primarily a tent city. When it went bust, the miners moved the tents to new claims. Even in more substantial towns with wooden buildings, it wasn't unusual to completely move the buildings to a new area after the town went bust.

In general, the most common extant ruins in Death Valley include mill ruins, metal or stone mine buildings, mine openings, and metal water towers. There are few mercantile or residential structures remaining (Rhyolite and Aguereberry Camp being two exceptions). The best-preserved towns are post-1950s company mining camps (Ibex Springs, Broken Pick, Warm Springs, Keystone Mine, etc.)

In this portfolio, I have defined several different types of ghost towns:

- **DEAD:** Meaning that the former mining camp or town is completely deserted, and has no inhabitants or businesses. Chloride Cliff is an example.
- **GHOST OF ITS FORMER SELF:** Meaning that the population has decreased radically since the boom days, with just a few

hardy souls keeping it alive. Ballarat and Rhyolite are examples.
- **ARRESTED DECAY:** Meaning that a governmental or corporate body is attempting to prevent further decay of the site. Harmony Borax Works is an example.

Throughout this study, I have used a personal rating system (0 low; 10 high) to rank three categories in each ghost town. These include:

- **REMAINS:** What is the quantity and quality of remaining boom-days structures in the town or area?
- **ACCESSIBILITY:** How easy is it to get to the site?
- **EXPLORING:** How accessible are the buildings in the town? Posted "No Trespassing" areas are rated low; open areas in National Forests/Parks are rated high.

The book is divided into two basic parts – East Side and West Side. Roughly, Badwater Road and Scotty's Castle Road provide the east/west divider. The sites referenced herein are not limited to the physical boundaries of Death Valley National Park, but rather are focused on sites associated with Death Valley mining. Ballarat, for example, isn't within the Park boundaries, but it is certainly associated with Death Valley mining.

The vast majority of the photos in this book were taken in the 21st century. Thus, this book focuses primarily on what there is to see in the Death Valley ghost towns today, as opposed to extensively examining the history of the sites (although I'll do a bit of that, also, along the way).

I hope this little photographic study proves interesting to fans of these lonely reminders of our American heritage.

- Robert Jones, Kennesaw, Georgia

Death Valley – East Side

Amargosa Borax Works

Founded:	1884/1888
Ghost town type:	Dead
Mining type:	Borax
Location:	About 5 miles S of Shoshone on SR127
Remains:	2
Accessibility:	10
Exploring:	10

Background

Amargosa Borax Works was owned and operated by William T. Coleman under the auspices of the Harmony Borax Mining Company. During the heat of the summer in 1884-1888, borax production was moved here from Harmony Borax Works in Death Valley. 20-mule teams were used to transport borax to the railroad from this site.

What is left to see
Two tiny adobe walls.

Ashford Mine (Golden Treasure Mine)

Founded:	1907
Ghost town type:	Dead
Mining type:	Gold
Location:	From Ashford Mill – travel E on Ashford Canyon Rd. for 3 miles, and then hike about 1.25 miles up Ashford Canyon to the mine site (2200 ft. altitude). Try to follow the remnants of the old road up the Canyon, when possible.
Remains:	8
Accessibility:	1
Exploring:	10

Background

The Ashford Mine (a.k.a. Golden Treasure Mine) was originally started by the three Ashford brothers, Harold, Henry and Louis. It was the *raison d'etre* for the better-known today (and much easier to access) Ashford Mill. The mine started producing gold as early as 1907, but it was never a big producer. It operated with 50 men from February-September 1915, when it closed down, as all of the high grade ore had been mined.

The Ashfords later leased the mine to Golden Treasure Mines, Inc., which mined the property from 1935-1938. Some time in the late-1930s or early 1940s, the Ashfords leased the mine to Bernard Granville and Associates of Los Angeles, who were notable for erecting a short tramway on the property. There are remains of this tramway extant today.

What is left to see

While you have to really want to get to this site (the 1.25 mile hike climbs 1100 feet up a difficult canyon), it is well worth it when you arrive. There are three standing buildings, as well as well as an ore chute and other mining remains. Also – a spectacular view of Death Valley from the hill above the outhouse.

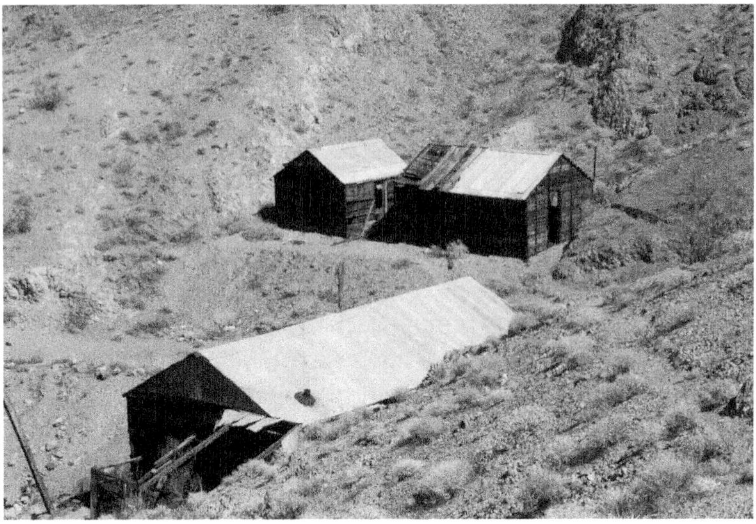

Bonnie Claire

Founded:	1904 (Thorpe's Well); renamed Bonnie Claire in 1906
Population:	1907: 100
Ghost town type:	Ghost of its former self
Mining type:	Gold milling; railroad center; later, lead smelting
Location:	About 20 miles NE of Scotty's Castle on SR72/SR267
Remains:	10
Accessibility:	10
Exploring:	10 (however, posted private property) in years past)

Background

Lippincott Smelter

A miner named Guy Thorpe mined this area in the late 19th century. After his death in 1893, a friend of Guy Thorpe's, Louis Chiatovich, started large scale mining operations in 1896. In 1905, Los Angeles real estate entrepreneur Willis Emerson headed a group which purchased an interest in the mine. The name of their company was the Bonnie Clare Bullfrog and Mining Company. The "Bonnie" part of the name came from the first name of Emerson's wife.

Bonnie Claire served as a station on the Bullfrog & Goldfield and Las Vegas & Tonopah railroads from 1906–1928. It served as a shipping center during the construction of Scotty's Castle in the 1920s. The tracks were torn up and the post office closed in 1931.

Lippincott Smelter, across the road from the old town site, smelted lead ore from the Lippincott mine from 1935-1953. The Montana Station Mill operated at the old townsite in the late-1990s.

What's left to see

Significant ruins from Lippincott Smelter, including mill ruins, a barracks, and other out buildings. Across the road are the remains of the Montana Station Mill Site, which I believe is on the site of the original Bonnie Claire. In the past, both sites have been posted private property, but when I was there in 2007, both signs were gone.

Montana Station

Bullfrog

Founded:	1905
Population:	1906: 1,000
Ghost town type:	Dead
Mining type:	Gold
Location:	Just west of Rhyolite, NV (the turnout is marked on the road to Rhyolite)
Remains:	3
Accessibility:	10
Exploring:	10

Background

Bullfrog was essentially a suburb of the larger Rhyolite. It only functioned as a town from 1906-1909. Famous prospector Shorty Harris and his fellow prospector Ed Cross discovered gold nearby in 1904, and the Original Bullfrog Mine was founded. They took ore samples to nearby Goldfield, which was assessed at $700 a ton (!) In the ensuing gold rush, both Bullfrog and Rhyolite were formed. Both Shorty Harris and Ed Cross eventually sold out their claims, Shorty Harris for perhaps as little as $500.

Both Rhyolite and Bullfrog were decimated by the financial panic of 1907.

This 1905 photo of Bullfrog shows what is largely a tent city[1]

What's left to see

Remains of the Bullfrog Ice House, and what might have been a jail (or a tourist attraction) behind a closed coffee shop.

---

[1] Library of Congress http://www.loc.gov/pictures/item/2007662539

Bullfrog Ice House

Carrara

Founded:	1904 (town site – 1913)
Ghost town type:	Dead
Mining type:	Marble
Location:	8.75 miles S of Beatty, NV on US 95 (the cement plant is visible from the highway)
Remains:	8
Accessibility:	10
Exploring:	10 (except townsite)

Background

Marble quarrying began in the area as early as 1904, with a town site dedicated in 1913. The Post Office closed in 1924. In 1936, a cement company built several buildings near the old town site, but never began operations.

Ruins of the Carrara cement plant, with US 95 in the background

What is left to see

Ruins of several stone buildings (associated with the 1936 cement company). Sparse remains of the Gold Ace Mine further up the hill, and of the old town site a mile to the south:

> "Carrara is about 1+ mile south of the Cement Plant ruins. It is marked by a large, partly sawed slab of marble. The tramway went up from there. You can see three quarry sites at the top, though on my last run, there was wire across the road and signage. Both the LV&T and then the T&T ran spurs to the marble cutting. The town site is about 2/3rds of the way up. Many foundations and marked building flats, plus debris". (John A. McCulloch)

Chloride Cliff

Founded:	1872, 1905
Ghost town type:	Dead
Mining type:	Silver, gold, lead, cinnabar
Location:	East-central side of Death Valley; 14 miles SW of Beatty
Interesting features:	Sweeping view of Death Valley
Remains:	2
Accessibility:	3
Exploring:	10

Background

Silver mining was started in this area in 1872 by A. J. Franklin, a civil engineer employed by the U.S. Government. The pack route he defined between his mine and San Bernardino was later used by the 20 Mule Teams operating from Harmony and Amargosa Borax Works.

In 1905, because of recent finds at Bullfrog and Keane Wonder Mine, operations restarted around Chloride Cliff by companies including the Bullfrog Cliff Mining Company and the Death Valley Mining and Milling Company. The first town site was created in this era. The revival was short-lived, as the financial panic caused by the San Francisco earthquake was especially devastating to the Chloride Cliff mines.

In 1910, a small mill was installed by the Pennsylvania Mining and Leasing Company, but an adequate water supply was lacking. By 1917, all mines in the area were idle.

Mining continued in the area off and on into the 1940s, including a cinnabar (mercury) mine that operated briefly in 1941.

What is left to see

A few mine openings, scant mill ruins; a water tank several miles to the NW. Almost nothing of the 1905 town remains.

Remains near the original 1872 Franklin Mine

Death Valley Junction

Founded:	1907
Ghost town type:	Ghost of its former self
Mining type:	Borate
Location:	On California SR127, about 7 miles S of the Nevada state line
Remains:	10
Accessibility:	10
Exploring:	5 (some private property)

Background

Death Valley Junction was created primarily as a railroad town, existing at the confluence of the Tonapah and Tidewater Railroad (which ran roughly north and south), and the Death Valley Railroad (that went west to the mines at Ryan). At it's peak, before the mines at Ryan closed in 1927, about 100 people lived there. Today, it is closer to 20. The two most famous buildings in the town – today the Amargosa Hotel and the Amargosa Opera House – were built by Pacific Coast Borax c. 1923.

What is left to see

Various old buildings and ruins associated with Pacific Coast Borax, and the T&T and DV railroads.

This page shows the postmasters in Death Valley Junction in the 1930s and 1940s. For some strange reason, the post office insisted on calling the town "Death Valley", instead of "Death Valley Junction". On the original post office application, the word "Junction" is repeatedly crossed out. Harry P. Gower was a longtime employee of Pacific Coast Borax, and was manager of the T&T ranch at one time. (National Archives)

Gladstone Mine

Founded:	1879
Ghost town type:	Dead
Mining type:	Gold
Location:	In the Ibex Wilderness, just east of Death Valley National Park
Remains:	5
Accessibility:	2 (6.5 mile round trip hike)
Exploring:	10

Background

The Gladstone Mine is part of the Ibex Wilderness, located just east of Death Valley National Park. The Wilderness was created as part of the 1994 Desert Protection Act, and now has 28,804 acres. It is administered by the Bureau of Land Management.

The Gladstone Mine was probably connected to the Gladstone Gold and Silver Mining Company, established in June 1879 by Barton O'Dair, John S. Thompson, and Amasa C. Kasson (see section on Kasson).

What is left to see

There is only one road in or out of the Gladstone Mine area. As one enters the "suburbs", one is greeted by three rock cairns on a hillside. Two of the cairns have what look like tombstones attached to them. Whether this is actually a burial ground (the hillside is very rocky), or they are just meant to greet the visitor to the greater Gladstone Mine area, I don't know.

As one walks around the hillside from the cairns, the first major structure is a multi-room stone building (no roof). Further on are several smaller stone buildings (all without roofs). At the top of the hill (and the end of the road) is an interesting cave and the ruins of a small stone building, seemingly connected (the cave has both a vertical and horizontal entrance).

The USGS map for this area shows the existence of a mill. (*The Thirteenth Report of the State Mineralogist for the Two Years Ending September 15, 1896* (California State Mining Bureau, J.J. Crawford, State Mineralogist, 1896)) report shows the existence of a steam mill in "Ibex", but not necessarily at this site). I not only didn't find the remains of a mill here, I didn't see any mine openings, either. It very much seemed like a small town site or mining camp to me. It could have been the original location of Kasson, although the remains are probably from a later date.

To see a map of the Ibex Wilderness:

http://www.blm.gov/pgdata/etc/medialib/blm/ca/pdf/pa/wilderness/maps_1page.Par.9668.File.dat/ibex.pdf

On the hillside, climbing towards the cave

Greenwater District

Founded:	1905 (post office closed in 1908)
Population:	1907: 2,000-2,500
Ghost town type:	Dead
Mining type:	Copper
Location:	Lower SE corner of the National Park, about 14 miles S. of the intersection of SR190 and Furnace Creek Wash Rd.
Remains:	2 (only in Kunze)
Accessibility:	4
Exploring:	10

Background

Copper was discovered here by Fred Birney and Phil Creasor in February of 1905. Quickly, claims were bought up by copper magnates including Patsy Clark, F. August Heinze, the "copper king" of Butte, Montana, and Arthur Kunze, of whom a town on the site would be named. By 1906, Charles Schwab of Bethlehem Steel fame was involved with the Greenwater Death Valley Copper Company.

This 1906 photo of Greenwater is part of a larger panoramic photo[2]

During the boom times, there were actually three town sites in the District – Furnace, Kunze, and Ramsey. Competition to be the preeminent town in the Greenwater District was especially fierce between the latter two. Kunze briefly had its own newspaper, the

---

[2] Library of Congress http://www.loc.gov/pictures/item/2007660637

Greenwater Times, and its own Post Office. In 1907, because of railroad interests, all three town sites were consolidated at the Ramsey site, which was renamed Greenwater. Two new newspapers sprang up – the *Greenwater Miner*, and the *Death Valley Chuck-Walla*.

Greenwater District never produced any ore of note. It was done in by issues endemic to Death Valley mining – fire, lack of water, and large transportation costs. And it turned out that most of the high grade copper was on the surface, and was quickly mined out. By the end of 1908, the boom was over. The Post Office closed on August 15, 1908.

R. J. "Dad" Fairbanks hauled several of the abandoned structures from Greenwater to Shoshone, and started a store.

What is left to see

The town sites of Furnace and Greenwater contain nothing but rubble. Kunze, which was the original site of Greenwater (before it's move 3 miles west to the Ramsey site in 1906), has more extensive ruins, including a stone dugout house.

1998 photo of stone dugout building in Kunze (named after Arthur Kunze)

Ibex Springs

Founded/abandoned:	1883: Mill site for Ibex Mine (silver) 1907: Mining Camp for silver mines 1950s & 1960s: Mining camp for nearby talc mines
Ghost town type:	Dead
Mining type:	Silver, talc
Location:	From a point on SR127 (at the microwave tower - about 2 miles S of the Ibex Pass), head 5.3 miles W
Remains:	10
Accessibility:	2 (4WD required)
Exploring:	10

Background

The Ibex Springs site as it exists today is a typical modern company mine camp, similar to Warm Springs or Broken Pick. Most of the extant buildings date from the talc-mining operations that began in the 1930s and continued into the 1960s. Two prominent names associated with this phase of mining at Ibex Springs were the Sierra Talc Company and Southern California Minerals Company. Prominent mines include the Monarch and the Pleasanton.

Two earlier iterations of the town (1883 and 1907) were to support nearby silver mines, the most prominent being the Lost Bethune Mining Company, established in October of 1906. The mine was named after Judge L. Bethune, who established a mine here in 1901. After his death from a drinking binge in 1905, his mine was briefly "lost", although it was rediscovered by 1906.

What is left to see

One of the most extensive extant ghost towns in Death Valley, with numerous standing buildings, and extensive talc mining ruins. Especially interesting is the area around the springs itself, which has an oasis-type feel .

Inyo Mines

Founded:	1905/1941
Ghost town type:	Dead
Mining type:	Gold
Location:	9 miles E of SR190 (12 miles from Visitor Center) on Echo Canyon Rd.
Remains:	10
Accessibility:	4
Exploring:	10

Background

Mining started in Echo Canyon as early as 1905, when claims were staked by Maroni Hicks and Chet Leavitt. Eventually the claims at the site were incorporated as Inyo Gold Mining Company. By 1907, three shafts had been sunk, and a gasoline hoist had been procured. The company decided to go public with its shares in 1907, just in time for the financial panic of 1907. Mining operations ended by 1912.

Mining operation started up again by 1938, as the Inyo Consolidated Mining Company. A ball mill was installed at the site in that year that could process twenty-five tons of ore per day. Operations continued sporadically until 1941, when all mining operations stopped.

What's left to see

Inyo Mine in Echo Canyon has some of the most extensive remains in Death Valley National Park. Several cabins, the remains of the mill, and an old diesel engine are extant.

Nearby is the town site of Schwab (nothing left except a flat area), which in 1907 was said to have a population of 200. Charles Schwab (Bethlehem Steel) at one time considered investing in Inyo Mines, but he never did more than kick the tires. Between Schwab and Inyo Mines are the remains of the Saddle Cabin (which is said to have been associated with Inyo Mine.)

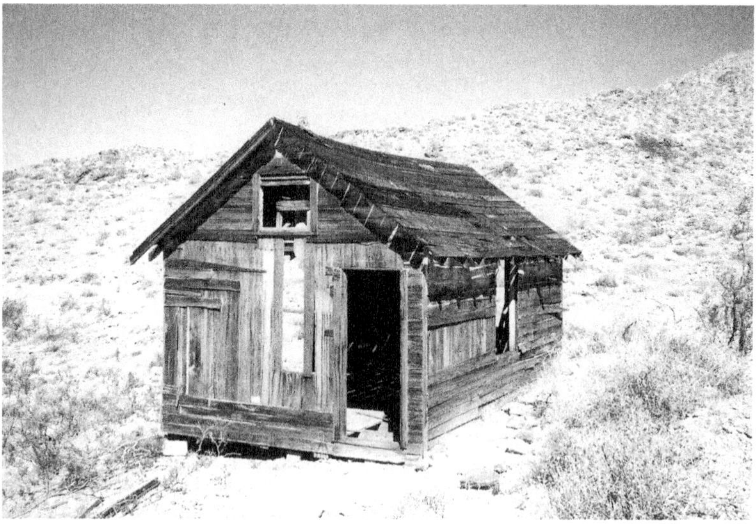

Kasson

Founded/abandoned:	1879
Ghost town type:	Lost (Dead)
Mining type:	Gold
Location:	"The name of the nearest office to the proposed one, on the same route is Tecopa. Its distance is 12 miles, in a north easterly direction from the proposed office." (National Archives)

Background

Like Leadfield and Greenwater, Kasson was essentially a stock swindle. According to Lingenfelter:

> Barton O'Dair had a claim called the Vulture, which he had opened with financial aid from Los Angeles attorney and city councilman John S. Thompson, among others. When they found the ore wouldn't pay, they decided to look for a buyer back East. They found just the man in Amasa C. Kasson, a Milwaukee sewing-machine salesman. Together they organized the Gladstone Gold and Silver Mining Company in June 1879, with $12 million in stock for sale.[3]

The *Report of Board of Trustees and State Mineralogist* for 1907/08 discusses stock swindles in general (not specific to Kasson):

> During the course of the Bureau's investigations into fraudulent oil and mining companies, it was found that, invariably, the capitalization was very large, the holdings in some case consisting of worthless mining locations; in others, of options to purchase, which options were never closed. In some instances, leases of no value were secured, but they served as a basis for the faker to operate on. Cases can also be cited where the corporations holdings were only on paper, and the stock buyers interests consisted solely of nicely engraved certificates.[4]

---

[3] *Death Valley and the Amargosa: A Land of Illusion*, by Richard E. Lingenfelter, p. 144

Like the supposed wealth of the claim, the town of Kasson existed mostly on paper. However, there was a post office there for several months in 1879, which was discontinued in November, 1879.

The original application form for the post office was signed by none other than the aforementioned John S. Thompson, listed as the "proposed post master".

Where was Kasson?

Kasson is a "Lost" ghost town today. It doesn't appear on any modern topographical maps, including the USGS. Some possibilities:

- Lingenfelter places Kasson about halfway (as the crow flies) between Tecopa and Saratoga Springs. By my reckoning, that would place Kasson just to the west of Sperry Wash, which can be found on the USGS maps of the area.
- An 1885 map of Inyo County, made available on the Inyo County GenWeb (http://www.cagenweb.com/inyo/maps.htm) shows Kasson as being south (and slightly east) of the Amargosa Mines (at Salt Spring)
- On old postal route map, sent to me by noted Death Valley and Mojave Historian Larry Vredenburgh, places Kasson to the west of modern SR127, at the point where the Amargosa River begins its U-turn into Death Valley. In modern terms, this would place Kasson several miles west of the SR127, off of the Harry Wade Road (Saratoga Springs Road, on some maps).
- Blair Davenport, the Museum Curator of Death Valley National Park, e-mailed me a reference from the November 1984 issue of *Desert Magazine*, which places Kasson "12 miles northwest of Tecopa". Interestingly enough, there is a mine (probably from

---

[4] *Report of Board of Trustees and State Mineralogist: Covering the Fifty-Eighth Fiscal Year Ending June 30, 1907 and Fifty-Ninth Fiscal Year Ending June 30, 1908* (W.H. Shannon Superintendent State Printing, 1908)

the 20th century) named the Gladstone Mine located...12 miles northwest of Tecopa.
- The national archives list of post office applications in Inyo County states "The name of the nearest office to the proposed one, on the same route is Tecopa. Its distance is 12 miles, in a north easterly direction from the proposed office." (National Archives) Note that the Tecopa referred to here is "Old" Tecopa, located near the Noonday Mine – not the 20th century railroad town located 8 miles to the West.

Keane Springs

Founded/abandoned:	1906/1909
Ghost town type:	Dead
Mining type:	Gold
Location:	Northeast portion of Death Valley. From Beatty, head West on SR374 for 15.8 miles. Turn left (East), and travel 2 miles to the road barrier on your left. Hike .75 miles down the barricaded road towards the big willow tree. (Note: the road goes to your right up a rise shortly after the barricade)
Remains:	1
Accessibility:	3 (requires .75 mile hike)
Exploring:	10

Background

Keane Springs existed as a small (mostly tent) town during the Rhyolite boom in 1906, mostly because of its water source, used by mines at nearby Chloride Cliff. In February 1906, a Death Valley

Mercantile Company store opened. The town was almost completely wiped out in a flood in 1909 (the town was actually built in the wash downstream from the spring!)

What is left to see

The only thing left is rusted pipe and some low stone walls. Note that the town remains are in the wash leading up to the spring/tree.

Keane Wonder Mine

Founded:	1903
Ghost town type:	Dead
Mining type:	Gold
Location:	Northeast portion of Death Valley
Remains:	7
Accessibility:	7
Exploring:	10

Background

In 1903, two prospectors named Domingo Etcharren and Jack Keane mined an outcropping of silver ore here, which eventually led to a rich gold vein. By 1906, the two prospectors had sold the mine outright to the Homer Wilson Trust Company. In 1906 and 1907, construction started on a mill and a 4,700 foot long "Riblet gravity tram". The mill is gone today, but remains of the tramway and the lower tramway building still exist[5].

In 1909, a cyanide processing plant went into operation, to extract gold from the extensive tailings on the site. Also in 1909, "Old Dinah" rode again for several months, hauling supplies from Rhyolite to Keane Wonder Mine. Old Dinah's days in revenue service ended on November 13, 1909 when she burst a boiler traveling through Daylight Pass.

By late 1910, 75 men were employed at the site. In 1912, the mine was sold to Philadelphia investors for $600,000, a move which temporarily inflated its stock price. By the end of 1912, though, operations at the mine ceased. Ore worth over $750,000 was mined here from 1907–1911.[6] Keane Wonder Company was sold at a sheriff's auction in November 1914. Operations started up again, but by 1917, had ceased. Mining operation started up again in 1935 under new owners, but were ended by 1937. The mill was

---

[5] Note: The tramway was reconditioned in the 1940s
[6] http://www.nps.gov/history/history/online_books/deva/section4b3.htm

dismantled and shipped to Los Angeles after that. Brief mining activities occurred in the early 1940s, and then ceased.

The nearby Cyty Mill, located 1.5 miles north of Keane Wonder Mine, was founded by Johnnie Cyty, known as ""Johnnie-Behind-the-Gat" because of his fondness for guns. The claim that Cyty developed was disputed, and in 1908, he was arrested for manslaughter of one of the men who also attested to ownership of the claim. Cyty was eventually acquitted because of conflicting testimony, and the possibility of self-defense.

The 3-stamp Cyty Mill began operations on October 14th, 1911, but the mine was never successful. In 1922, Cyty was a watchman for the closed Keane Wonder Mine.

Bottom tramway housing

What is left to see

Scattered ruins and rubble at the base of the mountain. Good remains of the 1400-foot tramway that goes up the mountain to the mine. Mine openings. Keane Wonder Springs and the Cyty Mill are about a mile to the north.

Ruins of Cyty Mill, located near Keane Wonder Springs (1.5 miles north of Keane Wonder Mine Mill)

Leadfield

Founded/abandoned:	1926/1927
Ghost town type:	Dead
Mining type:	Lead
Location:	Titus Canyon
Remains:	8
Accessibility:	5
Exploring:	10

Background

As early as 1905, lead and copper claims were staked in the Leadfield area. Mining occurred for several months, but ended because of high transportation costs. In 1925, Jack Salsberry established the Western Lead Mines Company, with over 50 claims in the Leadfield area. By early 1926, work on the town of Leadfield had begun, and half a dozen mining companies were in operation. In February of 1926, C. C. Julian, a California "oil promoter" became president of Western Lead Mines, and started heavily promoting the town and mines. On March 15, 1926, Julian sponsored what in modern terms might be called an "open house" at Leadfield, and over 1,000 people came to see the nascent boom town. Politicians made speeches, and a splendid time was had by all.

Leadfield continued to prosper and grow, A post office opened there on August 25, 1926. New mining companies continued to open up operations there, including the Pacific Lead Mines No. 2. By the end of 1926, though, C.C. Julian, Western Lead Mines, and the town of Leadfield were all broke (all of them being inexorably connected financially), for reasons having to do with the legality/illegality of the sale of Western Lead Mines stock. Other mining operations closed, too, and the still-standing Post Office closed in January 1927.

Leadfield Post Office

What is left to see
Several corrugated iron buildings, one dugout building.

Lee/Lee Annex

Founded/abandoned:	1907/1912
Population:	1907: 500
Ghost town type:	Dead
Mining type:	Gold
Location:	Take Amargosa Farm Road (paved) 10.9 miles W to Saddleback, and turn N. At Frontier Road, turn W, and then right almost immediately onto a tortuous dirt/rock road. Lee Annex is 2.9 miles, and Lee is 3.9 miles.
Remains:	2
Accessibility:	2
Exploring:	10

Background

Lee, California (sometimes "Lee's Camp"), Lee, Nevada and Lee Annex (sometimes "Lee Addition"), were competing gold boom towns around the same time as the Rhyolite boom.

The Lee, Nevada site was created in January of 1907 by the Lee Townsite & Mining Company. Soon after, the rival town of Lee, California was started by the Lee Hidden Treasure Mining Company. By February 1907, there were 150 people living in the two towns.

In April of 1907, the owner of the Lee Hidden Treasure Mining Company, S. J. Hernstadt, struck water about 3.5 miles from the Lee, CA site. He quickly built a pipeline to Lee, CA, ensuring that the California town would be the winner in the Lee sweepstakes. Soon, the population of Lee, CA was over 300, including 20 ladies.

A third competitor, sometimes called Lee Annex or Lee Addition, was established about a mile to the east of the original Lee, CA. A main attraction of this Lee was the fact that it wasn't developed in a wash like the original Lee, CA was!

By the Fall of 1907, the Tonopah & Tidewater Railroad was making noises about building a spur to the original Lee, CA. They even named a station on their Rhyolite mainline "Leeland", about six miles from Lee, CA. By November 1907, Lee, CA had a population of 500 – probably its peak. Soon after, though, the financial panic of 1907 caused mining operations to close and the town itself to start to dwindle. By 1912, the Post Office was moved to Leeland on the T&T Railroad. The town soon died after that.

c. 1908 panorama of Lee, California[7]

What is left to see

Numerous stone walls, cellar dugouts, and rubble over a wide area. The highest stone walls are about two feet tall, and are located midway between the two towns (N of the "main" road). Tailings at the Hayseed Mine. Note also the interesting stone bridge that crosses the wash that leads to the aforementioned structures.

---

[7] Library of Congress http://www.loc.gov/pictures/item/2007660688

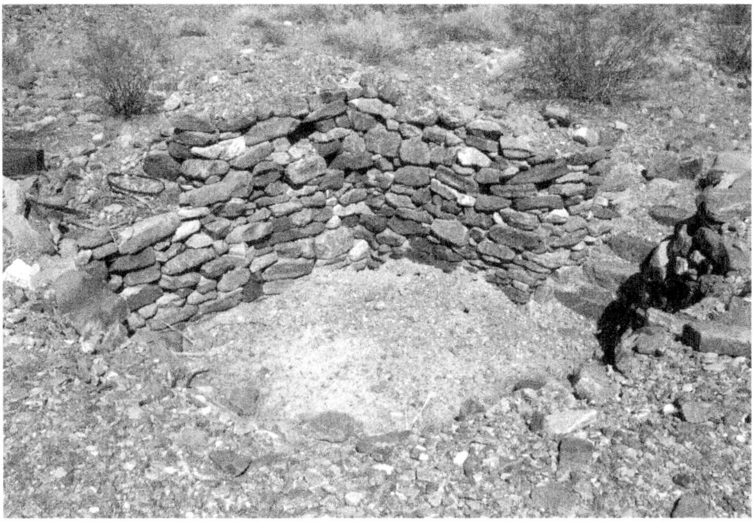

Lila C. Mine ("Old Ryan")

Founded/abandoned:	1907/1915
Population:	300 at peak
Ghost town type:	Dead
Mining type:	Borax
Location:	Take Hwy 127 1.2 miles S from Death Valley Junction. Turn W on dirt Petro Road for about 5.5 miles.
Remains:	2
Accessibility:	7
Exploring:	10 (private, but not posted)

Background

The original site of Ryan was at the Lila C. Mine. It operated from 1907 to 1915, and was abandoned when "New" Ryan, served by the Death Valley Railroad, opened in 1915.

What is left to see

Scant mill foundations, old water tanks, interesting concrete mine openings (or ventilation shafts?)

Longstreet Cabin

Founded:	c. 1895
Ghost town type:	Dead
Location:	Ash Meadows National Wildlife Refuge, Amargosa Valley, Nye County, Nevada (Look for "Longstreet Spring" on an Ash Meadows map. [8])
Remains:	10 (cabin has been restored)
Accessibility:	7
Exploring	10

Background

Jack Longstreet (1834-1928) settled in the Ash Meadows area in 1895, and built and lived in the cabin pictured below for several years. In 1899, he moved out of the cabin, and later sold the property in 1905. Longstreet was (at various times) a gunman, a farmer, a miner and a saloon keeper.

---

[8] http://www.fws.gov/desertcomplex/ashmeadows/map.htm

What is left to see

The Longstreet Cabin was rebuilt by the U.S. Fish and Wildlife Service in 2004/05 using as much of the original building material of the cabin as possible.

Monarch Canyon Mine

Founded:	1905
Ghost town type:	Dead
Mining type:	Gold
Location:	Northeast portion of Death Valley. From Beatty, head West on SR374 for 15.8 miles. Turn left (East), and travel 2.2 miles. Follow the road to your right down into Monarch Canyon, until the road disappears. Hike about a mile further down the canyon, through the sea of (very stiff) reeds. The mill remains will be on your left.
Remains:	4
Accessibility:	2 (requires 1 mile hike through rugged terrain)
Exploring:	10

Background

Monarch Canyon mine operated in the 1905-1910 era, founded by A. K. Ishmael. A one stamp mill was built in 1910, making use of plentiful water further up Monarch Canyon The mill was not operated regularly after October 1910, possibly because the ore was already running out.

Monarch Canyon Mill (1910) (Photo by Debra Kasson-Jones)

What is left to see

Pretty much all that is left are the interesting remains of the mill, which cascades down the mountainside.

Rhodes Spring

Founded/abandoned:	1885, 1950s
Ghost town type:	Dead
Mining type:	Mill site, spring, silver
Location:	On Jubilee Pass Road, 16.6 miles from Hwy 127, turn N on unmarked dirt road, and head 1.2 miles to springs. Take the left fork that appears soon after turning off Jubilee Pass Rd.
Remains:	5
Accessibility:	9
Exploring:	10

Background

A. G. Rhodes and his partner discovered this site c. 1886. They mined the site briefly, but gave up because of high transportation costs. J. Irving Crowell and the Bonanza Greenwater Company operated several mines at Rhodes Springs in 1905-1907, making no more than a small profit (although the transportation picture had improved somewhat since 1886). The financial panic of 1907 may have negatively impacted mining in the Rhodes Springs area.

A small mill operated at Rhodes Springs, probably in the 1930s-1950s.

What is left to see

For a site so close to a paved road, Rhodes Springs has some well-preserved remains. The most stellar example - a wonderful miner's cabin originally built in the 1930s, that still has covers on the mattresses, and functional kitchen and tableware. Also at the site - a metal shed, a concrete water tank, and various mill rubble.

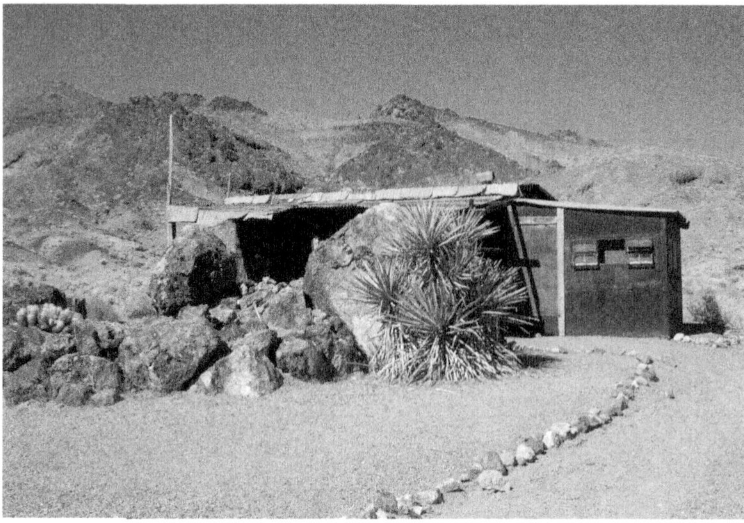

Rhyolite

Founded/abandoned:	1905/1922
Population:	1907: 6,000 1910: 675 1922: 1
Ghost town type:	Ghost of its former self; active mining operations nearby
Mining type:	Gold (3.1 million dollars from 12 mines)
Location:	1.5 miles N of Rt. 374, near Beatty, NV
Remains:	10
Accessibility:	9
Exploring:	7

Background

Rhyolite is one of the most famous ghost towns in the old west, because of the large number of extant buildings. Gold was originally discovered in the area by famous Death Valley prospector Frank "Shorty" Harris in 1904. By 1907, there were four newspapers, three railroads, as well as a number of profitable mines and mills (one owned by Charles Schwab). The financial panic of 1907 caused the boom town to go bust.

c. 1907 photo of the Montgomery Shoshone Mill in Rhyolite[9]

What is left to see

Several streets are fairly intact, and there are impressive remains of a bank, school, jail, retail store, and the Las Vegas & Tonopah

---
[9] Library of Congress http://www.loc.gov/pictures/item/2007662528

Railroad station. Also, the famous 1906 bottle house, made out of thousands of beer and champagne bottles can be seen here.

John S. Cook Bank

HD & LD Porter Mercantile, 1906, grossed $150,000 per month before the 1907 financial panic

Rhyolite School

Jail

The famous "Bottle House", made from thousands of beer and champagne bottles (1906)

Ryan

Founded/abandoned:	1915/1930
Population:	1927: 250
Ghost town type:	In stasis
Mining type:	Borax
Location:	4 miles S of SR190 (12 miles SE of Visitor Center)
Remains:	10
Accessibility:	8
Exploring	0 (private property)

Background

Actually the second site of Ryan, this one was operated from 1915/1930 by the Pacific Coast Borax Company. This was the rail head of the Death Valley Railroad, which ran to Death Valley Junction. After operations closed in 1927, the company briefly operated the Death Valley View Hotel as a resort, closing in 1930. The baby gauge railroad which ran from the mines to the town was operated as a tourist attraction until c. 1950.

The *Report XVII of the State Mineralogist: Mining in California during 1920* gives this description of Ryan and its mines:

> The main camp, called Ryan, is at the Biddy McCarty Mine, twenty miles north of west of Death Valley Junction. The Death Valley Railroad, a narrow gauge controlled by the same company, connects Ryan with Death Valley Junction. Ore trains operated by gasoline motors haul ore from the different mines to the main storage bins at Ryan...The ore from the different mines is segregated into first and second class ore, the first grade ore is shipped direct to the refineries at Bayonne, New Jersey, or Alameda, California, while second class ore goes to concentration plant at Death Valley Junction.[10]

---

[10] *Report XVII of the State Mineralogist: Mining in California During 1920* (California State Printing Office, 1921)

What's left to see

There are extensive remains at Ryan, all of which are on private property.

Salt Spring Hills (Amargosa Mines)

Founded/abandoned:	1850/1939
Ghost town type:	Dead
Mining type:	Gold, silver, lead
Location:	To the east of SR127, just south of where SR127 intersects Harry Wade/Saratoga Springs Road
Remains:	6
Accessibility:	6 (requires a hike)
Exploring:	10

Background

The mines at Salt Spring Hills, located on the Old Spanish Trail, are the first mines worked in the Death Valley area. In 1849, members of a wagon train headed by Mormon Brigade veteran Jefferson Hunt discovered gold at Salt Spring Hills, and mining operations began there as early as 1850. Operations continued on and off for the next 80 years or so, but it is said that no one ever made a profit, because of the remoteness of the area.

Remains of 1880s stamp mill

The Amargosa House – "This may be the oldest standing structure in the Mojave Desert. The three room office/house was originally constructed between 1850-1852." (Plaque at the site)

What is left to see

The remains of an 1880s stamp mill; the remains of the Amargosa House; mine openings; water tanks; rubble. There is a nice interpretive trail, leading from the parking area to the mines, as well as to an outstanding picnic area nestled in a grove of athel trees

Saratoga Springs

Founded/abandoned:	1883-1888: Water stop for the 20 Mule team wagons out of Amargosa Borax Works 1900s: Nitrate mining 1930s: Saratoga Water Co. resort
Ghost town type:	Dead
Mining type:	Nitrate, talc
Location:	From SR127 at Harry Wade Road – 5.8 miles West, then about 4 miles north
Remains:	1
Accessibility:	5 (bad washboard road)
Exploring:	10

Background

Saratoga Springs was discovered at least as early as 1871, and was named after Saratoga Springs in New York. It served as a watering stop for the 20 mule teams out of the Amargosa Borax Works. There were attempts at nitrate mining in the area in the early part of the 20th century.

The heyday of Saratoga Springs was in the 1930s, when talc mining started in the area. The Springs served as a prime water source for the mines. A small resort was also built at the Springs, and a number of buildings were erected. The resort died during World War II, and the mines played out in the 1960s.

Today, the pools at the spring cover 15 acres, and support exotic (for Death Valley) animals such as egrets.

What is left to see

Two stone foundations, probably dating to the late 19th century; signs of nitrate and talc mining on the hills to the north.

Saratoga Springs

Scotty's Castle

Founded:	1922
Ghost town type:	Residence
Location:	Northern part of Death Valley, in Grapevine Canyon
Remains:	10
Accessibility:	10 (paved roads from both the Nevada and California sides)
Exploring:	10 – grounds; 5 – castle (guided tours)

Background

"Scotty's Castle" (real name: Death Valley Ranch) was the desert hideaway mansion of Chicago insurance magnate Albert Johnson. Serious construction started in 1925, and continued into the 1930s (stopping for a while in 1931 while it was decided whether or not Death Valley Ranch had been built within the boundaries of the proposed Death Valley National Monument.) Johnson's insurance company went into receivership in 1933, a victim of the Depression, and work on the 8,000 square foot house was never completed.

While Johnson was the money man behind Death Valley Ranch, the site is most closely associated in the public mind with Walter Scott,

"Death Valley Scotty", a local flimflam man that Johnson happened to like. While it is sometimes said that Scotty never actually lived at the ranch, he had a bedroom there, and he also sometimes slept in the (ornate) kitchen. After Johnson's death, Scotty lived out the rest of his life at the castle.

Grave of Death Valley Scotty

The site is administered today by the National Park Service.

What is left to see

The mansion; construction debris; Scotty's grave; various out buildings.

Shoshone Caves

Founded/abandoned:	1907/1970s
Ghost town type:	Dead
Location:	Dublin Gulch, Two blocks W of SR127 in Shoshone, CA
Remains:	10
Accessibility:	10
Exploring:	10

Background

The Shoshone Caves are one of the unheralded marvels of the Death Valley area. The caves, carved into the rock of nearby cliffs, served as the homes of Death Valley miners and prospectors during the early part of the 20th century. There is a story about one miner (Joe Volmer, 1858-1938) who bought a natural gas-powered refrigerator for his cave, but was never able to procure propane in such a remote area. He ended up using it as a storage cabinet.

The town of Shoshone itself was founded on April 18, 1910 by Ralph "Dad" Fairbanks, an Amargosa Valley entrepreneur, who had founded a small settlement in Ash Meadows named Fairbanks. In the 1920s, Charles Brown (1884-1963), the son-in-law of Dad Fairbanks, took over ownership of the town from his father-in-law, who had moved on to new business opportunities in Baker. In 1938, Charles Brown became a California State Senator – a post he held for 24 years.

What is left to see

About ten undisturbed "cliff-dweller" homes created and used by Death Valley miners. Also in the Gulch – the Shoshone cemetery, which contains graves of Dublin Gulch miners, as well as the grave of State Senator Charles Brown and his wife.

Residence of Henry Ashford, of Ashford Mill and Ashford Mine fame

Ralph "Dad" Fairbanks owned a silica mining claim in this area, according to the *Report XVII of the State Mineralogist: Mining in California During 1920*.

> Shoshone Silica Deposit. The deposit is located ¼ mile west of Shoshone, a station on the Tonopah and Tidewater railroad. Holdings consist of two placer claims, 320 acres, recently purchased from R. J. Fairbanks of Shoshone. Elevation 1,700 feet. In low hills on the western side of Amargosa Valley, beds of silica 8 feet think occur in the Pleistocene sediments.[11]

In Shoshone itself - many old mining/RR buildings, plus the old General Store, a restaurant built in the late 1930s and an old motel.

---

[11] *Report XVII of the State Mineralogist: Mining in California During 1920* (California State Printing Office, 1921)

Miner's Caves in Dublin Gulch (south side)

The Red Buggy Restaurant, now the Crowbar, was built in the late 1930s. Our wedding party ate there the night before our wedding in Pahrump in 2004

Both Charles Brown and his wife Stella served as postmasters of Shoshone in the early days. (National Archives)

Strozzi Ranch

Founded/abandoned:	1931/1947
Ghost town type:	Dead
Economy:	Ranching
Location:	From between mile-marker 71/72 on U.S. 95 (N of Beatty), travel 19 miles east on a dirt road, taking the left fork at 12.2 miles.
Remains:	8
Accessibility:	3
Exploring:	10

Background
Caesar Strozzi built this ranch in 1931 to use for cattle/goat grazing and raising chickens.

What is left to see

One of the unheralded great spots in DVNP. Strozzi Ranch has several standing buildings, including two cabins, and some chicken coops. In addition, there are two picnic tables and a porta-potty (curiously marked "Men") located above the ranch. The site is lush (for Death Valley), and relatively cool at 6,200 feet.

Tecopa Mines

Founded/abandoned:	"Old Tecopa" – 1875; Tecopa - 1907
Ghost town type:	"Old Tecopa" – Dead; Tecopa – still alive and well
Mining type:	Lead/silver
Location:	Southeast of Shoshone, East of SR127
Remains:	10
Accessibility:	"Old" Tecopa – 5; Tecopa - 10
Exploring:	8 (some private property)

Background

"Old" Tecopa grew up near a group of mines collectively known as the Noonday Mines in 1877. The mines operated on and off into the 1950s. The Tecopa Railroad once linked the mines to the Tonopah and Tidewater Railroad. The *Report XVII of the State Mineralogist: Mining in California During 1920* has this entry for Tecopa:

> Noonday and Grant Mines. (Lead, silver, zinc). Located in Resting Springs district, 9 miles southeast of Tecopa and 2 miles southeast of the Gunsite mine. Elevation 2880 feet. Spur track of the Tonopah and Tidewater Railroad to mine from Tecopa...Second class ore, 4 to 5% lead and 4 to 6 ozs. silver goes to concentration plant at Tecopa. Thirty-five men employed at mine. Mill capacity 100 tons per day. Treating 60 tons.[12]

---

[12] *Report XVII of the State Mineralogist: Mining in California During 1920* (California State Printing Office, 1921)

Café/bar/trading post in downtown Tecopa

Tecopa as we know it today, eight miles to the west of the old town site, grew up in 1907, when the Tonopah and Tidewater Railroad came through. Tecopa is the site of the famous Tecopa Hot Springs.

Remains of the Anaconda Mill in the Noonday Mines area. The Mill operated 1946-1957. The photo above was taken in 2007, the one on the previous page in 1999. Note the deterioration of the site.

What is left to see

There are significant mining ruins in the Noonday mining district. There are many interesting old buildings in modern Tecopa.

Above two photos: Mine remains from the Grant Mine in the Noonday Mines area. In 2007, I rescued three twenty-somethings whose Jeep battery had died at this location.

Downtown Tecopa: Morgan Brothers maintenance building (l), and the old T&T Railroad freight depot (r).

To people passing by Tecopa on SR127, this is probably the most noticeable part of the town. The structure on the left was used for ore from the Noonday Mine. The structure on the right was used for talc from local mines (probably to the west).

Entering China Ranch, which sells dates. The sign commemorates the "Acme Siding" (1915) which used to run from the Tonapah & Tidewater RR main line through China Ranch to the Gypsum Queen Mines. A listing in the *Report XVII of the State Mineralogist: Mining in California During 1920* states "Acme Cement and Plaster Company. Resting Springs district. Large deposit of gypsum on China or Morrison Ranch, one mile northeast of

Acme Station on the Tonopah and Tidewater Railroad. Elevation 1500 feet. The company owns four claims known as the Gypsy Queen group."[13]

---

[13] *Report XVII of the State Mineralogist: Mining in California During 1920* (California State Printing Office, 1921)

Death Valley West Side

Aguereberry Camp/Eureka Mine/Harrisburg

Founded/abandoned:	1905/1945
Population:	1905: 300 (Harrisburg)
Ghost town type:	Dead
Mining type:	Gold
Location:	On the west-central side of Death Valley, between Skidoo and Wildrose Spring
Remains:	10
Accessibility:	7
Exploring:	10

Background

The two most famous prospectors in Death Valley mining lore, Shorty Harris and Pete Aguereberry, found the gold strike at Harrisburg in 1905. A town called Harrisburg, in honor of Shorty Harris, briefly blossomed. By 1906, the tent city of Harrisburg had vanished, as miners flocked to the new finds at nearby Skidoo. However, significant mining activity continued in the area until 1910.

Pete Aguereberry continued to mine his Eureka Mine until his death in 1945. In later years, it is said that he made more money giving tourists guided mine tours than he did from actual mining.

What is left to see

Harrisburg has entirely vanished, as it was mostly a tent city. However, the remains of Pete Aguereberry's camp and mining operation (Eureka Mine) are among the most well preserved ghost town remains in Death Valley. Beds, refrigerators and stoves remain in place as if Old Pete just stepped out for a trip to the local store. Cashier Mill is more or less intact, and the stabilized Eureka

Mine is sporadically open for exploration (it has been closed in the past in support of the local bat population).

Cashier Mill (c. 1917)

Argenta Mine

Founded:	1924
Ghost town type:	Dead
Mining type:	Silver, lead
Location:	From Emigrant Junction on State Highway 190, travel about 13 miles S on Emigrant Canyon Road. On your left will be a road that heads back to a small maintenance area. A dirt road heads to the NE just as you enter the maintenance area. Take that road about a mile, and you'll see the Argenta Mine ruins (Alternate route – drive down the wash from the end (NE) of the maintenance yard, until you see the mine ruins)
Remains:	5
Accessibility:	8 (high clearance)
Exploring:	10

Background

Operations started here in 1924, and continued through the 1920s, first by the Rainbow Mining Company, and then by the Southwestern Lead Corporation. An employee of the latter company, George G. Greist, sued the company into foreclosure in 1930 over the issue of unpaid wages. Greist was able to buy the mine, and operated it on and off (sometimes through lessees) until 1950.

There may have been a 19th century mine by the same name.

What is left to see

Foundations of numerous buildings; several old cars; a large water tank; mine openings.

Argenta Mine

Ashford Mill

Founded/abandoned:	c. 1915 (mine established 1907)
Ghost town type:	Dead
Mining type:	Gold
Location:	Southern part of Death Valley, 25 miles E of Shoshone
Remains:	5
Accessibility:	10
Exploring:	10

Background

Ashford Mill was established c. 1915 to process ore from the nearby Golden Treasure Mine (a.k.a. Ashford Mine). Curiously enough, the mill shut down after processing a few tons of ore, and was never reopened.

The mill site is easily accessed, as it is about 100 yards off of Route 178.

What is left to see

One concrete mill building; concrete pilings from the mill.

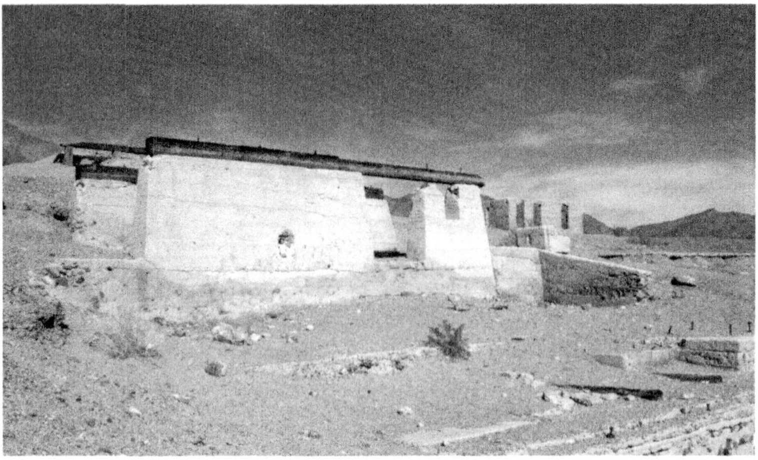

Ballarat

Founded:	1897
Population:	c. 1900: 400/500
Ghost town type:	Ghost of its former self
Mining type:	Gold
Location:	Outside of the Park boundaries, on the western side
Remains:	7
Accessibility:	5
Exploring:	3

Background

'49ers camped near here on their way to California, probably at nearby Post Office Spring. Ballarat itself was founded in 1897, named after the famous mining district in Australia. The main mine there, the Radcliffe, operated from 1898 to 1903. The post office closed in 1917, but sporadic mining activity occurred in the 1927-1942 era, mostly cyanide reduction of tailings from the Radcliffe.

Prospector "Shorty" Harris lived in Ballarat in the 1930s, and died there in 1934. The last resident of old Ballarat, "Seldom Seen Slim" died in Ballarat in 1968, and is buried in the cemetery there.

Ballarat was briefly inhabited by Charles Manson and his "family" in 1969.

What is left to see

Ballarat was completely dead for a period after the death of its last resident in 1968, but there are several residents now, and a small "General Store" which caters to tourists. There are several intact, abandoned buildings (made mostly out of wood and clay), as well as a maintained graveyard. Ballarat is often the embarkation point for the 10 hour round trip hike to the ghost town Panamint City.

"This was the home of Fred Grey – Assayer, miner and honorary mayor of Ballarat. He lived here 51 years. He had a college education (USC) in mining, engineering and assaying." ("Lightfoot Louie", town caretaker)

Charles Manson's truck – abandoned in Ballarat in 1969

School house – "The first school marm was Mrs. Mary Bigelow for the first and only school year 1899-1900. Frank "Shorty" Harris lived here several years before his death in 1934." ("Lightfoot Louie")

Assay Office, used by Fred Grey. Charles Manson's "family" stayed in this house briefly before leaving for the Barker Ranch in 1969.

Ballarat Jail/Morgue. According to "Lightfoot Louie", the building was built in 1900 for $336.50.

Barker Ranch

Ghost town type:	Dead
Location:	A little over 21 miles from Ballarat (south on Wingate Road for 15 miles, then east up Goler Wash)
Remains:	10
Accessibility:	3 (recommend 4-wheel drive up Goler Wash, although the "falls" have been much improved recently)
Exploring:	10

Background

Not all of the myths and legends about Death Valley have to do with Argonauts and miners from long ago. In October of 1969, well within the living memory of many of us, Charles Manson and his "family" were apprehended in two raids at the Barker Ranch on the outskirts of Death Valley.

The Barker Ranch in 2007. A fire in May of 2009 caused damage to this structure.

Manson and his followers had moved into the area as early as summer of 1968, and sporadically inhabited the Barker Ranch and the nearby Myers Ranch (owned by the grandmother of one of the "family" members). Curiously, Manson met several times with Mrs. Barker, who lived at Indian Ranch, north of Ballarat. She had given her permission for Manson to use the Barker Ranch, but of course wasn't aware of the crimes committed by Manson and his family.

The first of the two raids occurred on October 10, 1969, when a combined force of National Park Service Rangers, California Highway Patrol officers, and representatives from the Inyo County district attorney's office launched a quasi-military raid on the Barker Ranch. Among the 13 people (mostly women) captured in the raid was Lynette "Squeaky" Fromme, who would later try to assassinate President Gerald Ford (September 5, 1975). The second raid occurred on October 12, 1969, and involved National Park Service Rangers, California Highway Patrol officers, and deputy sheriffs from Inyo County. Among those captured in this second raid was the leader of the "family", Charles Manson. He was found hiding under a vanity in the small Barker Ranch bathroom. No shots were fired, and no one was hurt during the two raids.

Ironically, Manson and his followers were not apprehended for the Tate/LaBianca/Hinman murders, but rather for the arson of a Death Valley "Michigan Articulating Loader" near the Lippincott Mine a month before (as well as various auto theft, stolen property and firearms charges). It wasn't until mid-November of 1969 that the "family" became prime suspects in the aforementioned murders (one jailed "family" member had spilled the beans to her cell mates).

In time, Manson and various family members would be convicted of 9 murders, and sentenced to death or life imprisonment. In June of 1972, the U.S. Supreme Court temporarily ended the death penalty and all death sentences were commuted to life imprisonment.

For an in depth account of the capture of Manson and his "family", see the indispensable *Desert Shadows: A true story of the Charles*

Manson Family in Death Valley by Bob Murphy (Sagebrush Press, 1993).

What's left to see

The Barker Ranch today is pretty much intact[14]. The kitchen and dining room still have furniture in them, and the famous bathroom where Manson was apprehended is still intact (although the vanity is gone). The kitchen also has a set of shelves that contain notes from various people who have visited the site over the years. One recent note stated that "I just wanted to see if I could figure out what was in Charlie's mind". A nearby bunkhouse made of railroad ties remains in good shape. The site also has a picnic table.

One of my favorite features of the Barker Ranch are the two signs pointing to rest facilities – if you follow them, they lead to an outdoor toilet with no walls. Luckily, the Barker Ranch is in a particularly isolated part of Death Valley.

The road to the Myers Ranch is closed, and it is posted private property.

A note on the directions: As you climb Goler Wash and near the top, you'll pass the large, abandoned Keystone Mine on the right. About 1.2 miles past that, you'll make a hard left through Sourdough Spring. After climbing the short hill, take the road to the right to get to the Barker Ranch, not the road that has the DVNP sign.

---

[14] A fire destroyed the main building in May 2009

The bathroom where Charles Manson was captured

Broken Pick/Trail Canyon

Founded:	1950s
Ghost town type:	Dead
Mining type:	Tungsten, antimony
Location:	9.5 miles W from the West Side Road, in Trail Canyon
Remains:	10
Accessibility:	1
Exploring:	10

Background

Mining activity started in Trail Canyon as early as 1906, with the creation of the Death Valley Wonder Mining & Milling Company, the Wild Rose Mining Company, and the Trail Canyon Mining Company. These efforts failed during the financial panic of 1907.

2,060,000 pounds of antimony were mined in Trail Canyon during World War I and World War II[15]. Tungsten mining started up in Trail Canyon after World War II, and continued into the 1950s. Broken Pick Mine and Millsite was part of the Tungsten mining boom.

What's left to see

At Broken Pick, some of the more substantial "town" remains in Death Valley National Park, including several buildings, an abandoned mobile home, and an outhouse with an intact toilet seat.

---

[15] http://www.nps.gov/history/history/online_books/deva/section3a16.htm

View of several remaining structures at the Broken Pick site

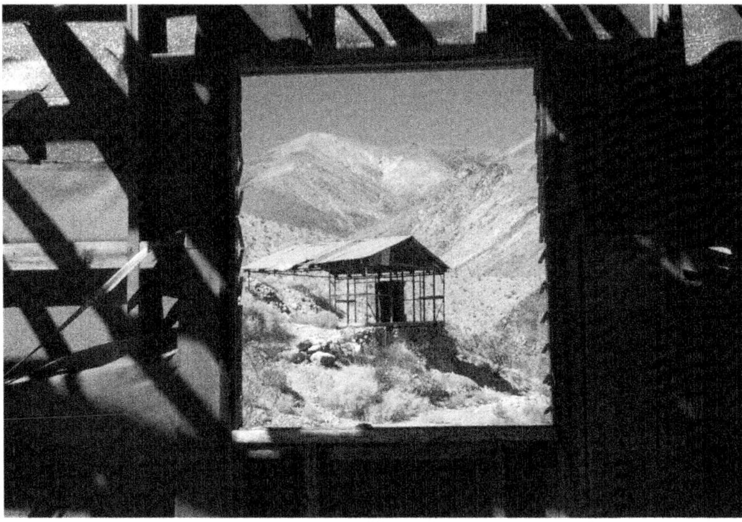

Christmas Mine

Founded/abandoned:	Late 19th century – 1970s
Ghost town type:	Dead
Mining type:	Silver
Location:	From Emigrant Junction on State Highway 190, travel about 17.4 miles on Emigrant Canyon Road. You'll see a dirt road going off to the east. Take this road about 1.6 miles until you see the outhouse.
Remains:	3
Accessibility:	6 (high clearance – 4WD would be helpful in a few spots)
Exploring:	10

Background

Silver mining occurred here on and off from the 19th century to the 1970s.

Collapsed bunk house

What is left to see

A two-seater outhouse; the roof frame of a cabin; an abandoned cyanide canister.

Corona Mine (Jail Canyon)

Founded:	1899 (Gem Mine)
Ghost town type:	Dead
Mining type:	Gold
Location:	From the intersection of Trona-Wildrose and Indian Ranch Roads, head SE on Indian Ranch road for about 4 miles. Turn left on the 4WD road to your left. (If you pass Indian Ranch, you missed the turn.) Drive about 6 miles up the 4WD road, which dead ends at the Corona Mine.
Remains:	10
Accessibility:	2 (bad 4WD road up the alluvial fan, and into Jail Canyon)
Exploring:	10

Background

Mining was started here in 1899 (by Jack Curran, according to a sign at the site), with the first mine being known as the Gem Mine. The claim was also known at one point as the New Discovery Mine. By 1951, the site was known by the name it still bears today – Corona.

What is left to see

There is much left to see for those hardy enough to make it up Jail Canyon to the Corona Mine. There are two standing cabins (and one collapsed one). The larger of the two cabins is still "camp-able", and has been cleaned up and repaired in recent years. In the mine camp area, there is also a trailer, a couple of abandoned trucks, a spring, picnic tables and much debris. Further up the side canyon are extensive mill ruins, complete with abandoned railroad tracks.

The main cabin in the Corona Mine camp

Inside the main cabin

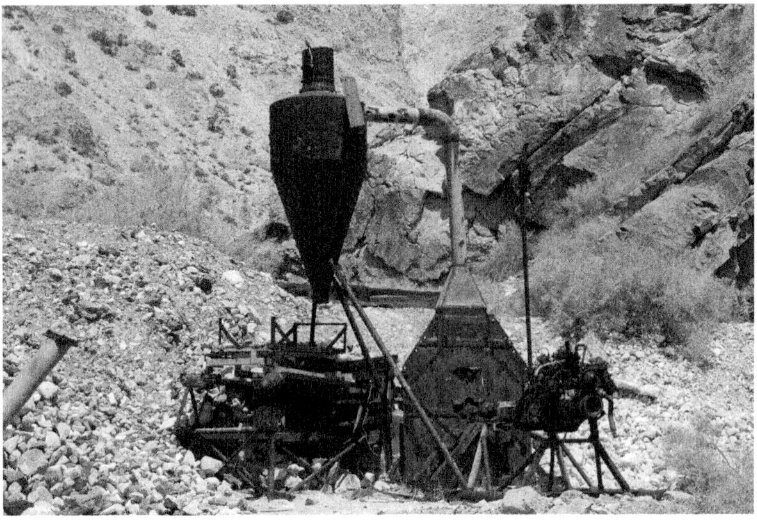

Crater

Founded:	1917: Deposits discovered; 1929: mining begins
Ghost town type:	Dead
Mining type:	Sulfur, mercury metal
Location:	In the extreme northern part of Death Valley National Park, in the Last Chance Range. From the end of the paved road near Ubehebe Crater, travel 27.9 miles north/northwest on what is noted as Big Pine Road on some maps, and Death Valley Road on others. You'll pass Crankshaft Junction on the right on the way. Crater is 7.3 miles west of Crankshaft Junction.
Remains:	8
Accessibility:	5 (mostly dirt, but graded). The first 10 miles from the paved road end near Ubehebe Crater is often washboarded. Watch your gas.
Exploring:	10

Background

Crater has been mined on and off since 1929, and at one time had a small town. It is said to be the largest deposit of sulfur west of the Mississippi. In 1930, there was talk of building a railroad (Pacific Sulfur Railroad) to the site from the west, but nothing ever came of it. In 1953, sulfur dust ignited and destroyed the mill.

In the 1990s, large scale sulfur production occurred on the site by American Sulfur, Inc. of Big Pine. Because the site was privately owned, it was not included in the confines of Death Valley National Park in 1994. There have been recent efforts to include Crater in Death Valley National Park.

What is left to see

There are several small buildings, and various mine openings scattered around a large area. Rusting tanks and machinery are scattered across the landscape. All of the current remains date from the 1990s and later.

Note that if you take the dirt road west of the mining area visible from the road and head north, you'll find other remains along the way, for about 3 miles. The road ends at the El Capitan mercury mine. 4WD is suggested. (On some maps, this road appears as Crater Road; on others, Sulfur Road).

Mine ruins at Crater

Crankshaft Crossing, 7.3 miles east of Crater. If you read in another book about the wonders of the Last Chance Cabin, located near Crankshaft Junction, resist the temptation to go to it. The cabin has collapsed, the road to it is horrible, and the last 200 yards is one of the most dangerous sections of road I've ever been on.

Darwin

Founded:	1874
Ghost town type:	Ghost of its former self (has a post office)
Population:	1877: 2,000 2000: 59
Mining type:	Silver, lead, zinc, copper
Location:	Just outside of DVNP on West-central side, 5.5 miles off of SR190
Remains:	10
Accessibility:	10 (paved road access)
Exploring:	2 (mostly private property)

Background

Founded in 1874 (Post Office, 1875), Darwin had a population of 2,000 by 1877. The silver mines declined soon after that, and Darwin declined. A second boom started around 1906, as copper lying in abandoned Darwin mine dumps rose in value. In 1945, the Anaconda Corporation took over most of the lead, silver and zinc mining in Darwin.

Old Darwin post office/store

From 1926-1937, Darwin was the western gateway into Death Valley, and experienced a small tourist boom. In 1937, SR190 was completed, bypassing the old mining town. The old road from Darwin to Darwin Falls is still passable, albeit in generally poor condition.

What is left to see

The main intersection in town – Main and Market Streets – has interesting buildings on all four corners, including an old post office, a dance hall, the old school, and abandoned residences.

According to the 2000 census, there are 40 occupied households in the town, with a total population of 59. There is an operating post office in Darwin.

The most interesting ruins are posted private property – the Darwin Mines property is being maintained for potential future mining operations. There are 20+ buildings on the Darwin Mine property, but they are not open for exploration.

Darwin Dance Hall (a.k.a. Miner's Union Hall, Crosson's Corner)

Old schoolhouse

Eagle Borax Works/Shorty Harris Grave

Founded:	1881
Ghost town type:	Dead
Mining type:	Borax
Location:	West Side Road, 12 miles from northern intersection with Badwater Rd.
Remains:	1
Accessibility:	7
Exploring:	10

Background

Isadore Daunet mined Borax here from 1881-1884. He eventually went bankrupt, and committed suicide in 1884.

What is left to see

A partially processed pile of borax. About half a mile from the Borax Works is the grave of famous Death Valley prospector Shorty Harris and his friend Jim Dayton.

Shorty Harris grave site

Galena Canyon

Ghost town type:	Dead
Mining type:	Talc
Location:	4+ miles W from the West Side Road, in Galena Canyon
Remains:	8
Accessibility:	4
Exploring:	10

Background

Galena Canyon has talc mine remains from four major mines, including the Bonney Talc Mine, the Mongolian Mine, the Mammoth Mine, and the Death Valley (White Eagle) Mine. The oldest of the mines is the Death Valley Mine, which saw mining activity as far back as 1929, mostly underground. Fairly rare for sites within Death Valley Monument, the other three mines were mostly strip mining operations, and operated in the 1950-1970s time frame. By the 1970s, all of the mines were owned by Phizer, Inc.

Death Valley Mine ore chute

Galena Canyon may have been the escape route for the 49ers saved by William Lewis Manly and John Rogers

What's left to see

Large tanks (one contained diesel fuel, one contained ammonium nitrate) of the Mammoth Mine, on a high cliff with a spectacular view of Death Valley; a small office (White Eagle Mine); an impressive ore-loading chute, that still has talc in the chutes (Death Valley Mine).

White Eagle Talc Mine office

Goldbelt

Founded/abandoned:	1904, 1915, 1950s
Ghost town type:	Dead
Mining type:	Gold, tungsten, talc
Location:	From Teakettle Junction, travel a little over 14 miles south on Hunter Mountain Road, and then look for one of two roads that head southeast toward Goldbelt Spring. Goldbelt is located less than a mile after turning off of Hunter Mountain Road.
Remains:	3
Accessibility:	4 (recommend 4-wheel drive)
Exploring:	10

Background

Gold was found near Goldbelt Spring in 1904 by famed Death Valley prospector Shorty Harris. Harris also discovered tungsten in 1915, and tungsten mines opened up in the area to meet the World War I demand. In the 1950s, a small talc mine operated near the spring.

One of the collapsed shacks (2007 photo)

What's left to see

The remains include three collapsed shacks, one dugout cabin, the remains of a water delivery system from the springs, a corral, and an abandoned vehicle. The shacks probably date from the 1930s or 1940s, but were also used by the talc miners in the 1950s. The nearby Calmet Mine has an abandoned metal ore (wollastonite) chute.

In the late 1980s, two of the shacks and an outhouse were still standing. All are gone or collapsed in 2007.

This 1987 photo by Michael Hirsch (from Berg am Irchel, Switzerland) shows two of the three shacks still standing. Michael's motorcycle broke down here in 1987 – a long way from anywhere!

Greene-Denner-Drake Mill

Founded:	c. 1952
Ghost town type:	Dead
Mining type:	Tungsten mill?
Location:	7.1 miles from SR190 on Emigrant Canyon Road. Look for a small turnout on the right side of the road, about .5 miles south of Journigan's Mill, and then hike about 1.4 miles up a small canyon to the mill site.
Remains:	8
Accessibility:	5 (About a 3-mile round trip hike)
Exploring:	10

Background

Not much is known about this mill site. It was originally built by Thad Greene, perhaps c. 1952. Greene had a small tungsten claim located on the road to Skidoo, so he may have built this mill to process ore from those claims. The mill was later owned by Erwin Denner and John Drake.

The mill was probably located here because of the nearby water source – Burns Spring.

What is left to see

The mill is still standing, as is a concrete bunkhouse. The bunkhouse still contains beds/bunks, chairs and a good size coal heater.

There are several water tanks, with the pipes running down from Burns Spring still visible. Several old cars, and a two-seater outhouse complete the scene.

Greene-Denner-Drake Mill in 2013

Greene-Denner-Drake Mill bunkhouse. You can just make out the water pipes running down from the spring above the top left of the structure. One of the water storage tanks is just visible to the right of the structure.

Harmony Borax Works

Founded/abandoned:	1882/1888
Ghost town type:	Arrested Decay
Mining type:	Borax
Location:	1.5 miles N of Furnace Creek Ranch
Remains:	5
Accessibility:	10
Exploring:	8

Background

William Coleman built and started operating the Harmony Borax Works in 1882. Borax, used as a cleaning agent for clothes, as well as other industrial purposes, was one of the main ores mined and processed in Death Valley. The Borax was scooped up from the Valley floor by Chinese workers, hauled to the Harmony Borax Works, and processed into borax crystals. From there, the crystals were hauled by the famous 20 Mule Teams to Mojave, 165 miles away. The Works shut down every summer, because the extreme heat in Death Valley interfered with the refining process.

What is left to see

The site is now maintained by the National Park Service, although it was originally preserved by the United States Borax & Chemical Corporation, a successor of the original owners. The shells of two outlining buildings can be seen, as well as remains of the mill itself. Two wagons and a water tank from an original 20 Mule Team stand on the site. Also, two-foot tall Borax "haystacks" still stand about 3 miles west of the site, on the Valley floor.

Borax and water wagons pulled by the famous "20 Mule Teams"

Coleman – the nearby town that housed the workers

"Old Dinah", a steam engine that was briefly used to haul ore to railheads. "Dinah" could travel 3.5 miles per hour, and broke down often! The engine is now located at Furnace Creek Ranch.

Hungry Bill's Ranch

Founded:	Mid-1870s
Ghost town type:	Dead
Economy:	Ranching
Location:	From the north end of the West side road, travel 20.9 miles south, and turn right (west) on Johnson Canyon Road. Head up the canyon until the road dead ends into Wilson Spring (about 10 miles). Hike up the canyon about 1.5 miles until you see the stone walls at Hungry Bill's Ranch.
Remains:	2
Accessibility:	1 (4WD)
Exploring:	10

Background

The land where Hungry Bill's Ranch is located belonged to the Timbisha Shoshones, until they were displaced by Swedish settlers in the 1870s. William Johnson (whom the canyon is named after) started a fruit and vegetable farm here around 1873, to provide produce to the miners at Panamint City, located about 6 miles away. The vegetable business was successful, but the fruit trees had probably not grown to maturity by the time Panamint City died, and William Johnson abandoned the ranch c. 1877.

The Wheeler Survey, conducted in 1876, describes what is probably Hungry Bill's ranch:

> The first portion of the descent to Death Valley by trail was very steep. In the canon through which we passed grass and a short running stream were found, also a small cultivated piece of ground where vegetables were raised with facility by irrigation. [16]

---

[16] http://www.nps.gov/history/history/online_books/deva/section3a14.htm

By 1891, the ranch had reverted to Timbisha Shoshone use, with an Indian named Hungry Bill inhabiting the site, along with various friends, family and associates. Hungry Bill applied for a homestead, which was granted by the United States Land Office at Independence on October 10, 1907.

Hungry Bill died in 1918 or 1919, and the ranch began to decay. The site came under control of the National Park Service on August 16, 1954. There are steps under way to create an Hungry Bill's Ranch Historic District.

What's left to see

The only thing left at Hungry Bill's ranch are some stone walls, a few trees, and some stone rubble that might have been a structure. At Wilson Spring (where you parked your car), there is a primitive picnic area. About .1 miles up the canyon (south side), there is an arrastre, and a second at .5.

As you hike up the canyon, you will quickly reach a point where further travel is impossible because of the thickness of the foliage. At this point, take to the canyon rim (south side). It is not an especially pleasant hike – you'll go up and down the canyon rim, the whole time looking down on the foliage in the canyon, which would provide a bit of shade, if you could actually get through it. At various points, you'll hear the sound of rushing water, which explains why the foliage is so dense in the canyon.

This arrastre is .1 miles north of the parking area at Wilson Spring (south side of canyon)

Hungry Bill's Ranch. Note the stone wall front/left.

Journigan's Mill

Founded/abandoned:	1937/1967
Ghost town type:	Dead
Mining type:	Gold mill (cyanide)
Location:	6.6 miles from SR190 on Emigrant Canyon Road
Remains:	6
Accessibility:	10 (all paved roads)
Exploring:	10

Background

There has been milling on this site from at least the 1920s. Shorty Harris is said to have operated a five-stamp mill here in 1924. Journigan's Mill was a gold mill (cyanide) that operated from 1937-1967. Its name came from its original owner, Roy Journigan, who had established the Journigan Mining and Milling Company. The mill was also known as the Gold Bottom Mill.

What's left to see

Two large chemical tanks, several concrete cyanide tanks, various rubble, including 4 old cars.

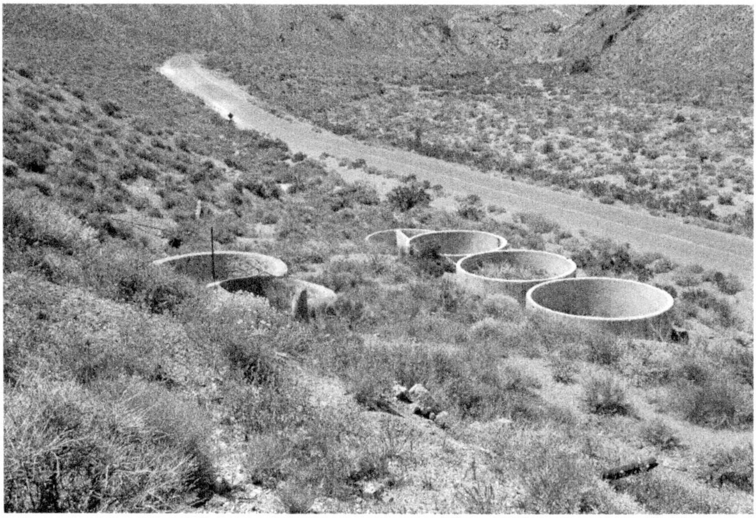

Keystone Mine (Lotus Mine)

Ghost town type:	Dead
Mining type:	Gold
Location:	About 19.4 miles from Ballarat (S on Wingate Road for 15 miles, then 4.4 miles east up Goler Wash)
Remains:	10
Accessibility:	3 (recommend 4-wheel drive up Goler Wash, although the "falls" have been much improved recently)
Exploring:	10

Background

The first mining in the area is said to have been done by Carl Mengel (a friend of Shorty Harris). In 1935, the property was acquired by Lotus Mines.

In the 1980s, the Keystone Mine operated a gold mine here. Most of the remains date from that later operation.

According to the Sierra Club website, the stone cabin is part of the BLM Adopt-A-Cabin Program, and is periodically fixed up by interested campers. There are also rumors that mining may begin again in this area.

What's left to see

Among the most extensive mining camp remains in or near Death Valley National Park (Keystone Mine is about 1.2 miles from the DVNP border). In the area just off of Goler Wash are several standing buildings, including the heretofore mentioned stone cabin. There are also 4 abandoned travel trailers, mill ruins, mining equipment, and much debris. Far up the canyon to the south is the actual entrance to the Keystone Mine. The mine had a 2,800-foot inclined rail-tram that carried ore down to Goler Wash.

There are various other mine camp ruins scattered along Goler Wash, including the (scant) remains of a circular 1920s gold mill site, the office (intact) of the Newman Mine, and remains of the cable tram from the Lestro Mountain Mine (located near Newman Mine Office).

Newman Mine Office

Lippincott Mine

Founded:	1906 (Lead King Mine)
Ghost town type:	Dead
Mining type:	Lead, silver
Location:	10 miles S of Teakettle Junction
Remains:	3
Accessibility:	2
Exploring:	10

Background

While this mine was founded in 1906, the largest operations occurred from 1942–1953[17] when the site was leased by George Lippincott of Goldfield, Nevada. The lead mined here was smelted at the Lippincott Smelter in Bonnie Claire, built in the early 1950s. Some mining activity continued at the Lippincott Mine into the 1970s.

This was also the site where Charles Manson and several of his followers torched a Death Valley National Park road grader in 1969.

What's left to see

An abandoned water truck, a washing machine, and wood and concrete rubble are all that mark this especially lonely site. The even sparser remains of the Homestake Mine can be found about a mile away near the Homestake Camping Area.

---

[17] The mine closed briefly during World War II because the area was used for aerial gunnery practice

Rubble at the Lippincott Mine

Lost Burro Mine

Founded/abandoned:	1907/1970s
Ghost town type:	Dead
Mining type:	Gold
Location:	About 4 miles W from Teakettle Junction
Remains:	7
Accessibility:	3
Exploring:	10

Background

The great name comes from a story that says that the original founder of the mine (Bert Shively) picked up a gold-laced rock in 1907 to throw at some stray burros. Heavy operations at this mine came and went in various decades, including 1912-1917, 1928, and the 1970s.

What is left to see

A wood frame cabin, a dugout cabin, mill ruins, and an outhouse. Note: The road from Hunter Mountain Road to this mine is in VERY bad shape.

Old Stovepipe Wells

Founded/abandoned:	late 19th century
Ghost town type:	Dead
Location:	North-central part of Death Valley, east of Stovepipe Wells Village
Remains:	2
Accessibility:	10
Exploring:	10

Background

During the late 19th and early 20th centuries, Old Stovepipe Wells was an important watering hole for Death Valley miners and prospectors. It is named for the length of stovepipe that was driven into the well, marking the site from shifting sands. Later, a small town was located here.

In 1926, "Bob" Eichbaum planned on making the site a winter resort. Because of difficulties in building a graded road to the area, he located the resort (the first in the Valley) several miles to the east (modern Stovepipe Wells).

Old Stovepipe Wells

What is left to see

Remains of the well; the grave of Val Nolan, who died in 1931 "a victim of the elements". One of the few known graves within Death Valley National Park.

Owl Hole Springs/Black Magic & New Deal Mines

Founded/abandoned:	Mines especially active during World I & II, and the Korean War
Ghost town type:	Dead
Mining type:	Manganese
Location:	About 22 miles W of SR127, on the Harry Wade and Owl Hole Springs roads
Remains:	2
Accessibility:	4 (22 miles of graded dirt road)
Exploring:	10

Background

Owl Hole Springs served as a mining camp for the nearby New Deal and Black Magic manganese mines.

What is left to see

Scant ruins at the Springs site; several mine openings and one stone foundation at the New Deal mine. A wooden ore chute, and the remains of terrace mining at the Black Magic Mine.

Owl Hole Springs

Panamint City

Founded/abandoned:	1873/1895
Population:	1874: 2,000
Ghost town type:	Dead
Mining type:	Silver
Location:	From Novak Camp (formally Chris Wicht Camp), a 6-mile hike east through Surprise Canyon, with about a 4,000 foot increase in elevation
Remains:	10 (including Surprise Canyon)
Accessibility:	1 (well, it is a 6-mile hike one-way)
Exploring	10

Background

Panamint City is one of the most famous of the Death Valley ghost towns. Silver was discovered here is 1873, and within a year, there were 2,000 people living in Panamint City. Two Nevada senators, William Stewart and John Jones were heavily invested in the Panamint City mining claims. The twenty-stamp Surprise Valley Mill/Smelter only operated for a couple of years in the mid-1870s, although mining continued on and off in the area until the end of the 19th century.

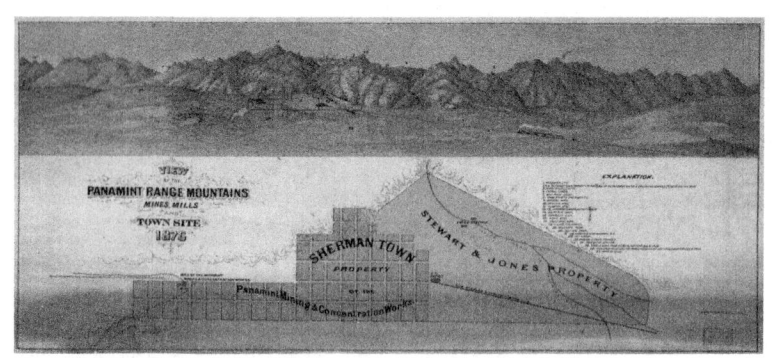

"View of the Panamint Range Mountains, mines, mills and town site ; Sherman Town, property of the Panamint Mining & Concentration Works" (1875)[18]

---

[18] Library of Congress http://hdl.loc.gov/loc.gmd/g4362p.mf000062

Panamint City is famous for the silver "cannonballs" that were cast at the smelter for transportation through Surprise Canyon. Because of their weight (several hundred pounds), it was impossible for bandits to steal them. The *Death Valley Days* episode "Bandits of the Panamints" tells the story well.

What is left to see

Periodic floods have destroyed many of the Panamint City and Surprise Canyon structures and roads over the years, including one in 1984 that destroyed the road through Surprise Canyon. Some 4-wheel drive vehicles were still able to navigate the road, until that was stopped in 2001 because of an environmental lawsuit.

There are remains of many interesting structures in Surprise Canyon, and at Panamint City, although the latter are spread out over a 1-mile+ area. The smokestack of the smelter is the most prominent. The hike through Surprise Canyon is one of the most spectacular hikes in Death Valley.

Queen of Sheba Mine/Carbonate

Founded/abandoned:	1908/1930 (Carbonate); 1924/1972 (Queen of Sheba Mine)
Ghost town type:	Dead
Mining type:	Silver (lead carbonate)
Location:	3.8 miles W of West Side Road, from Salt Well. Salt Well is located just south of the road to Galena Canyon.
Remains:	9
Accessibility:	5
Exploring	10

Background

Clarence E. Eddy found galena in the region in 1907. Carbonate Lead Mines were worked from 1908 to the early 1930s. The driving force behind the associated town was Jack Salsberry, who built a road between the mines and the Tonapah and Tidewater Railroad at Zabriskie. Part of the route still bears his name – Salsberry Pass. By the early 1920s, the mines were often idle.

By 1924, the name "Queen of Sheba" Mine appears, owned by New Sutherland Divide Mining Company, marking an area 1,500 feet southwest from the old mines at Carbonate. Mining continued there on and off, either by New Sutherland or lessees until 1949. Some mining activity started up again in the early 1970s at the site.

What is left to see

The remains at the Queen of Sheba include two shacks, extensive mill ruins, and an interesting ore shoot. There is extensive rubble over a wide area. Most of the structures date from the 1930s and 1940s.

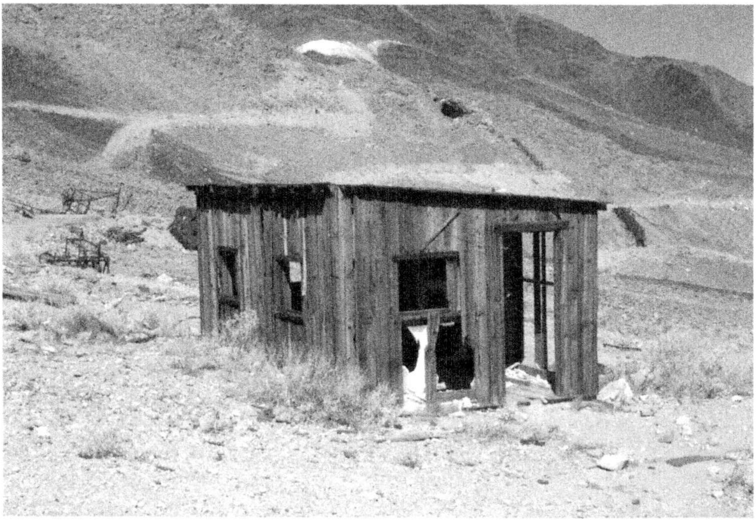

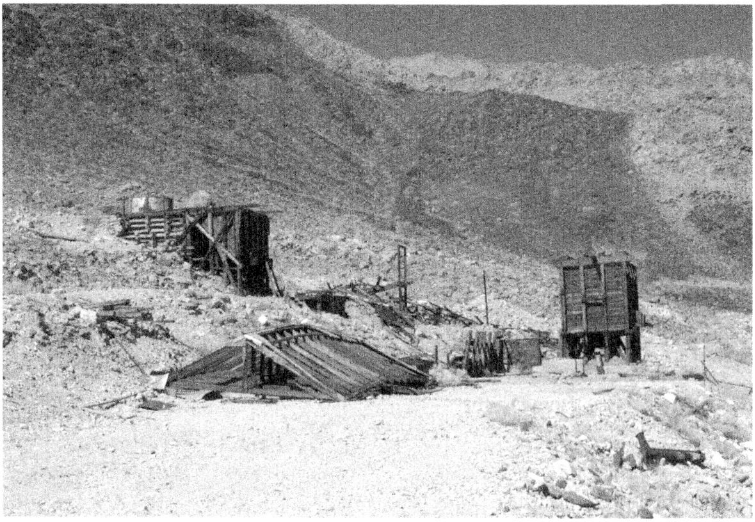

Skidoo

Founded/abandoned:	1906/1917
Population:	1907: 500
Ghost town type:	Dead
Mining type:	Gold
Location:	West-central part of Death Valley, accessed via a 14-mile dirt road
Remains:	5
Accessibility:	3
Exploring	10

Background

Prospectors John Ramsey and John "One Eye" Thompson discovered ore here in January of 1906, on their way to Harrisburg. Nevada promoter E. A. (Bob) Montgomery bought out their claims. By the end of 1906, Skidoo was beginning to thrive, and a Post Office was established there.

Founder Bob Montgomery wanted the town named after himself, although the Post Office originally called it "Hoveck", after Matt Hoveck, general manger of the Skidoo mines. Winnie Montgomery wanted to call it "Skidoo", and Winnie won out in the end over both her husband and the U.S. Government. The town may have been named after the phrase "23-skidoo", ostensibly because the nearest water supply was 23 miles away[19]. Another theory is that it was because Bob Montgomery filed 23 claims in the area.

A famous incident occurred in 1908 when Joe "Hooch" Simpson, a man of ill repute, murdered James Arnold, one of the founding father's of Skidoo, in the latter's store. The murderer was lynched by enraged townspeople several days later, on April 22, 1908.

The Skidoo mines proved remarkably resilient and profitable through much of World War I. However, on September 1, 1917, the

---

[19] A water pipeline from this source on Telescope Peak was completed in 1907, at an estimated cost of $250,000

ore ran out and the mines closed   By 1922, the population of Skidoo was one - "Old Tom Adams".

Mining revivals at Skidoo happened in the 1930s (with one of the owners being Roy Journigan, owner of the nearby mill). A tungsten mining boom started mining up in Skidoo again in the 1950s. Finally, there was some mining activity in the early 1970s, which included reopening the old Skidoo Mine from the early part of the 20th century.

These mill remains at Skidoo are on the National Register of Historic Places

What is left to see

There are no remains of the town, but extensive mill ruins can be found above the town to the west, with the masterpeice being the Skidoo Mines Company quartz stamp mill.

There are also various ruins along the 14-mile road to Skidoo.

Early 1950s cabin, on the road to Skidoo

Starr's Mill

Founded/abandoned:	1930s
Ghost town type:	Dead
Mining type:	Gold mill (cyanide)
Location:	5.4 miles from SR190 on Emigrant Canyon
Remains:	3
Accessibility:	10 (paved roads)
Exploring:	10

Background

This gold cyanide mill operated in the 1930s, processing ore from nearby Nemo Canyon. The operators were Walter M. Hoover and the man for whom the mill is name after – Starr (first name unknown).

What is left to see

Low stone walls, and cyanide tanks (the tanks are not visible from the road). Also, 100 yards south of Starr's Mill is Upper Emigrant Spring, which Bryan and Tucker-Bryan in *The Explorer's Guide to Death Valley National Park* identify as the location of the town of Emigrant Spring (1905/06). There are no remains of the town, but there is a small water flow from a pipe at the springs.

Stone walls at Starr's Mill

Tucki Mountain

Founded:	Discovered 1909
Ghost town type:	Dead
Mining type:	Gold
Location:	1.5 miles on Emigrant Canyon Road from SR190, then 9.9 miles on a 4x4 road
Remains:	8
Accessibility:	4
Exploring:	10

Background

One of the best 4x4 drives in DVNP (watch out for rock outcroppings at three places along the 9.9 mile route).

Gold may have been discovered on this site as early as 1909, but mining didn't start in any significant amount until 1927. Mining continued through the 1930s. The ubiquitous Roy Journigan became part owner of the mine in 1939. Operations ceased in 1951. The first period of production was from 1927-1951. The site was also mined in 1974/75 by descendents of Roy Journigan.

What is left to see

Several small buildings, including one that is stocked for emergency use (it contains canned food, tools, books/magazines, and even has a picture hanging on the wall). A perilous walk to the mine that overlooks the ghost town provides views of several mine openings with ore lift mechanisms, wooden ladders, and a small shack.

Shack stocked with emergency supplies

Ubehebe Mine

Founded:	Discovered 1875
Ghost town type:	Dead
Mining type:	Copper, silver, gold, lead
Location:	3 miles SW of Teakettle Junction
Remains:	6
Accessibility:	3
Exploring:	10

Background

Copper mining started in the Ubehebe mine in 1906. By 1908, the focus had changed to lead (galena), when an 8 foot thick seam was found. Archibald Farrington and two partners invested in the mine, and started the Ubehebe Mining Company. *Report XVII of the State Mineralogist: Mining in California During 1920* has an entry for Ubehebe Mine which states:

> Ubehebe Mine (Lead-silver). Ubehebe district, 52 miles by road southwest of Bonnie Claire, Nevada. Elevation 3930 feet. Idle. Arch Farington of Bishop, California, owner.[20]

During the teens and twenties, ore was transported to Bonnie Claire via a tractor, run by entrepreneur Frank A. Campbell. The area was busy and profitable, with a drop off in activity in 1929, as lead prices dropped.

Mining continued through the 1930s, and a tramway was built on the site (some sparse remains exist today). In the 1940 and early 1950s, zinc mining was added to the mix.

---

[20] *Report XVII of the State Mineralogist: Mining in California During 1920* (California State Printing Office, 1921)

What's left to see
One extant cabin, an interesting mine entrance, the remains of the tramway that once went up the mountain, and much rubble.

Warm Springs Camp/Gold Hill Mill

Founded/abandoned:	1931-1980s
Ghost town type:	Dead
Mining type:	Talc, gold
Location:	11 miles W of West Side Road (Warm Springs Canyon Road)
Remains:	10
Accessibility:	6
Exploring:	10

Background

Warm Springs Camp boasts perhaps the most intact mining camp remains in Death Valley. Significant mining in the area had its beginning between 1931 to 1935 when Louise Grantham and Ernest Huhn established claims in Warm Springs Canyon. The Gold Hill Mill was built c. 1939, and featured a diesel-powered arrastre. The Big Talc Mine started operating in 1942, and through 1959, was the biggest talc producer in the western United States.[21] During World War II, Warm Springs talc was used by the U.S. Navy for paint production.

Production at Big Talc and the other mines continued well into the 1970s, when Johns-Manville Corporation bought out all of the claims of Louise Grantham. They eventually closed because of ventilation problems in the underground mines, and a small amount of asbestos in the raw talc.

Warm Springs Camp itself was built by Louise Grantham to house workers in the nearby talc mines. In 1955, the Death Valley Monument superintendent called the Warm Springs Camp "finest mining camp of any in the Monument."[22] The camp was last used by Pfizer Inc. to house workers for the nearby White Point Talc Mine. It wasn't abandoned until the early 1980s.

---

[21] http://www.nps.gov/history/history/online_books/deva/section3a7.htm
[22] http://www.nps.gov/history/history/online_books/deva/section3a8.htm

Gene Park of McMinnville, Oregon worked at the mines here in the 1960s. He discusses the original owners of the camp and the building of the swimming pool at Warm Springs Camp:

> It was built by Louise Grantham and her Father. The mine was called Grantham Mines. I was working at the mine during the time the swimming pool was built as an equipment operator. This would have been around 1967-68. At that time we were mining out of "Big Talc" and " #5" mines that were about 2 miles east of the camp. The White Point Mine, if that is the portal just east of the camp, didn't exist when I was there and would have been built after Grantham sold out.

What is left to see

Extensive remains of the Gold Hill Mill remain, including a fairly intact arrastre. Warm Springs Camp is almost entirely intact, and includes several buildings (one with an impressive fireplace), a swimming pool (Warm Springs flows 5 gallons a minute), and garden tools left in place when the site was abandoned. There has been little deterioration at the site.

Warm Springs Camp swimming pool

c. 1939 Gold Hill Mill

Wildrose Canyon Kilns

Founded:	1877
Ghost town type:	Dead
Mining type:	Charcoal production
Location:	West-central part of Death Valley. From the intersection of Emigrant Canyon and Wildrose Canyons roads, head east on Wildrose Canyon Road for
Remains:	10
Accessibility:	7
Exploring	10

Background

The ten giant charcoal kilns at the mouth of Wildrose Canyon are still in perfect condition, over 100 years after they were built. The kilns produced charcoal for use by the lead ore smelting operations located at Lookout, 25 miles to the west.

Maps

The maps in this section show the relative locations of the sites discussed in this book, using existing NPS and BLM maps as a template. To find the full maps online (minus my additions), see:

http://www.nps.gov/deva/planyourvisit/upload/Backcountry-Roads-Map.pdf

http://www.blm.gov/pgdata/etc/medialib/blm/ca/pdf/pa/wilderness/maps_1page.Par.9668.File.dat/ibex.pdf

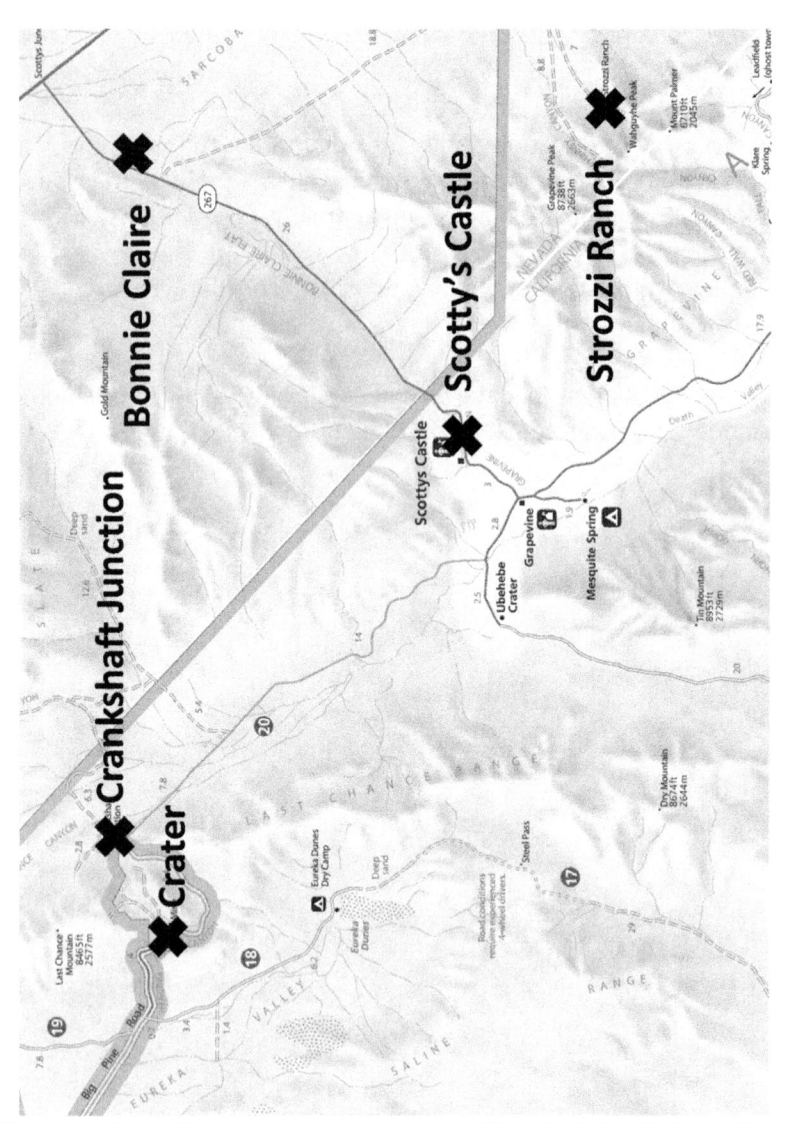

This map shows the extreme northern part of Death Valley National Park. Note that while Strozzi Ranch is shown on the map, the best way to get to it is from the east. (NPS map)

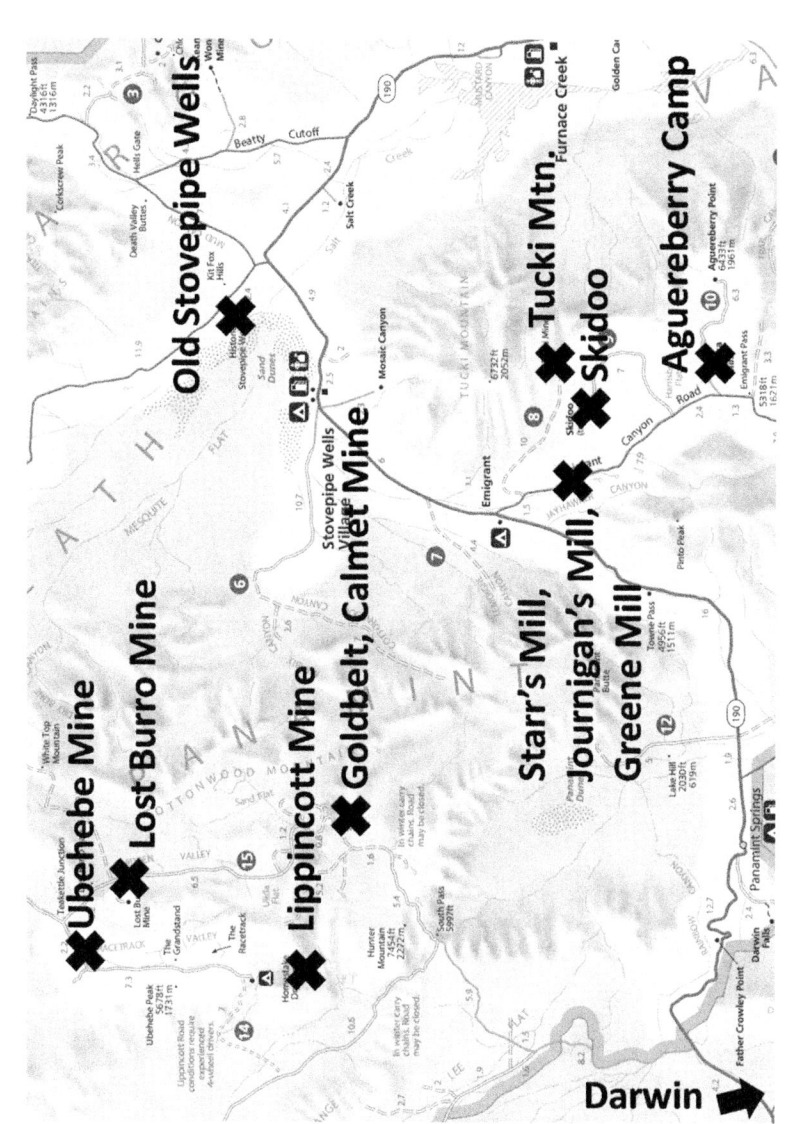

This map shows sites in the Racetrack and Emigrant Canyon Road areas
(NPS map)

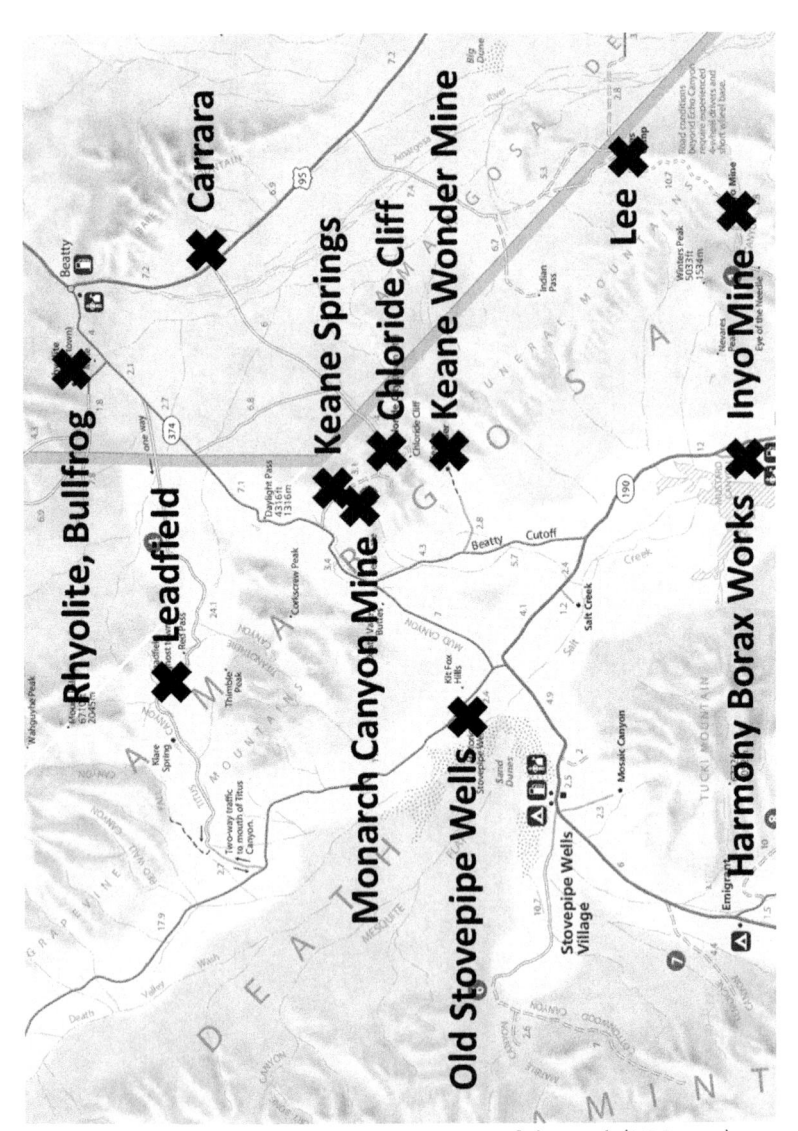

This map shows sites in the eastern part of the park (NPS map)

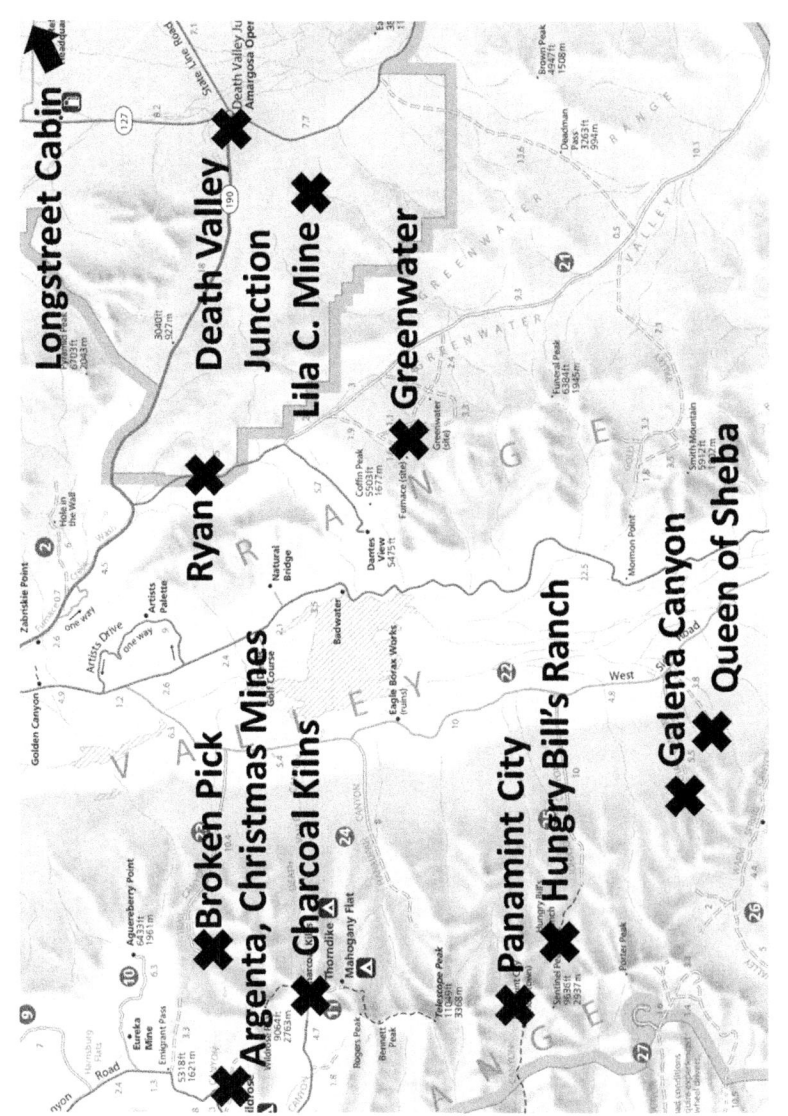

This map shows sites in the heart of Death Valley, and on the eastern slopes of the Panamints (NPS map)

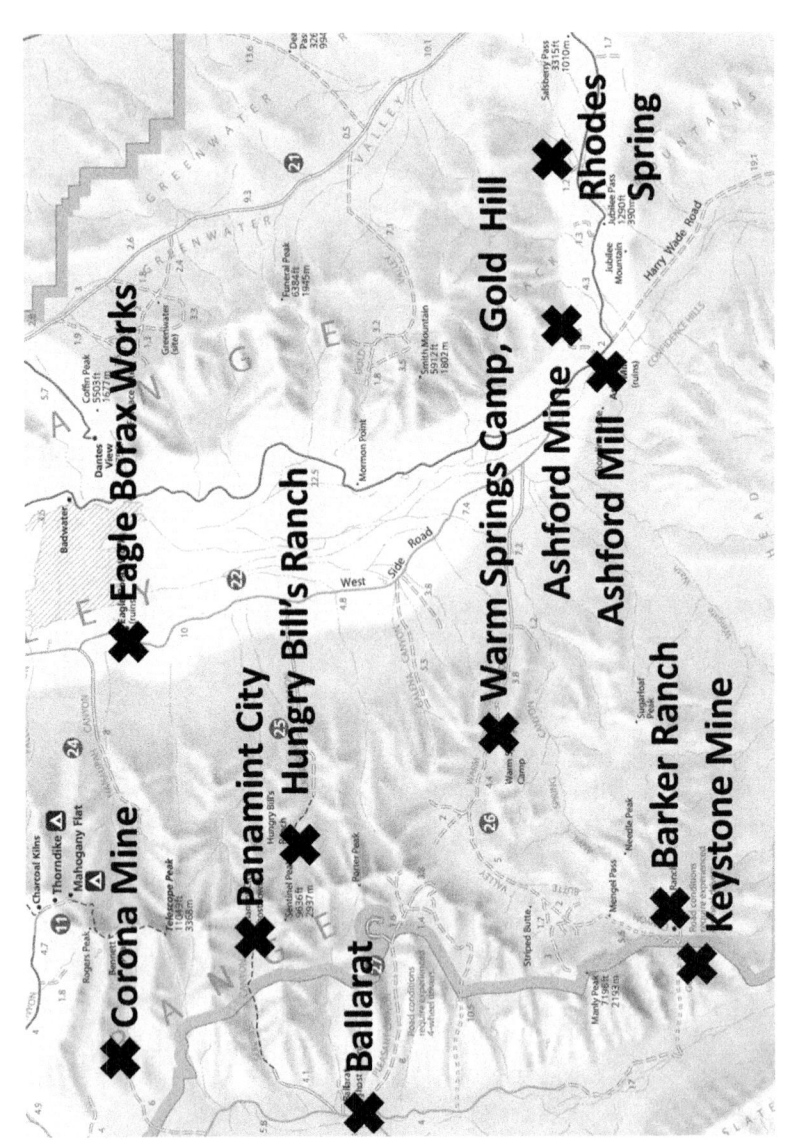

This map shows sites in and near the Panamints (NPS map)

This map shows sites in the southern part of the Park (NPS map)

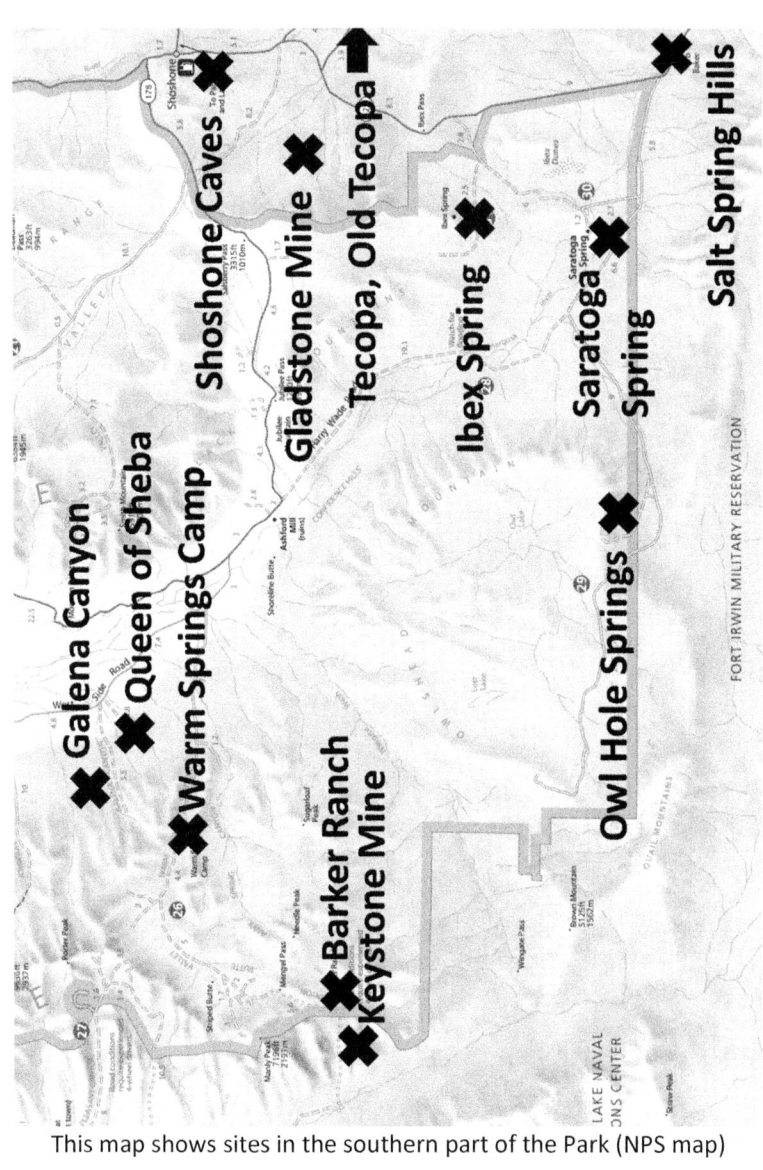

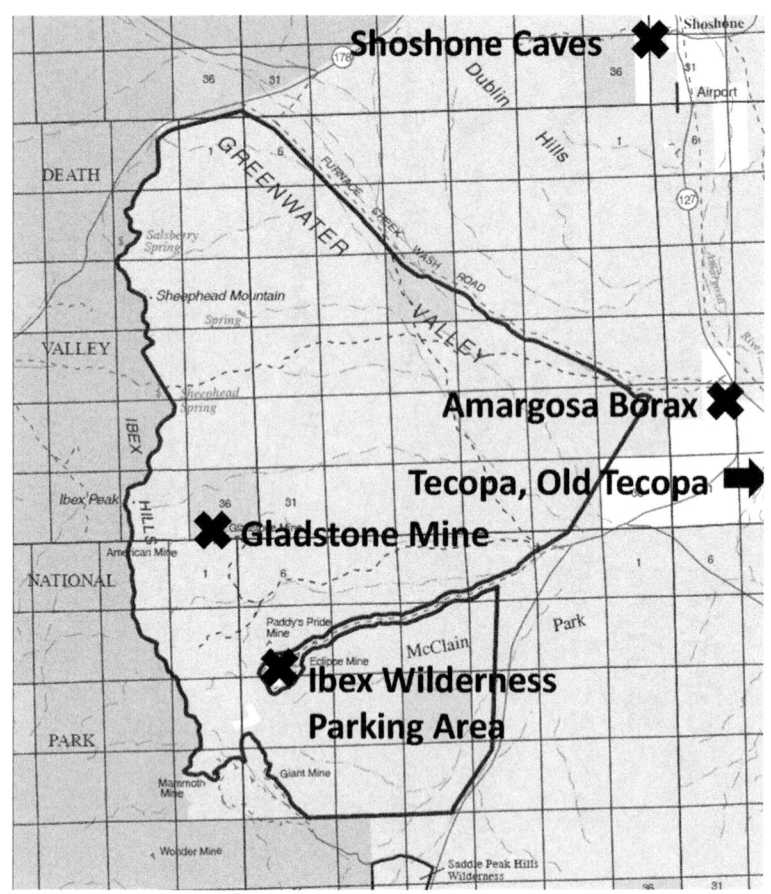

This BLM map shows the location of the Ibex Wilderness, and the location of the Gladstone Mine in relation to the parking area

Sources

- *Ballarat Town Layout*, "Map courtesy the General Store, Lightfoot Louie Mgr."
- *Darwin, California*, by Robert P. Palazzo (1996, Western Places)
- *Death Valley and the Amargosa: A Land of Illusion*, by Richard E. Lingenfelter (1986, University of California Press)
- *Death Valley Ghost Towns: Volume 1 & 2*, by Stanley W. Paher (1973, Nevada Publications)
- *Death Valley Historic Resource Study: A History of Mining*, Linda W. Greene, John A. Latschar, November 1979 (Study for the National Park Service)
- *Desert Shadows: A true story of the Charles Manson Family in Death Valley* by Bob Murphy (Sagebrush Press, 1993).
- *Early Shoshone and Tecopa Area* (Southeastern Death Valley Region), by Ken Lengner and George Ross (2004)
- *Explorer's Guide to Death Valley National Park, The* by T. Scott Bryan and Betty Tucker-Bryan (1995, University Press of Colorado)
- *Fort Irwin and Vicinity History of Mining Development*, by Larry M. Vredenburgh (1994, http://vredenburgh.org/mining_history/pages/fort_Irwin.html)
- *Hiking Death Valley*, by Michel Digonnet (2007)
- *Modern Pioneers of the Amargosa Valley, The* by Robert D. McCracken (Nye County Press, 1992)
- Post office records from the National Archives
- *Report of Board of Trustees and State Mineralogist: Covering the Fifty-Eighth Fiscal Year Ending June 30, 1907 and Fifty-Ninth Fiscal Year Ending June 30, 1908* (W.H. Shannon Superintendent State Printing, 1908)
- *Report XVII of the State Mineralogist: Mining in California During 1920* (California State Printing Office, 1921) – from Google Books
- *Tecopa Mines* by Ken Lengner & George Ross (2006)
- *The Thirteenth Report of the State Mineralogist for the Two Years Ending September 15, 1896* (California State Mining Bureau, J.J. Crawford, State Mineralogist, 1896)

Photos by Robert C. Jones, except as otherwise noted

The author at the Lippincott Smelter in Bonnie Claire in 2005 (Photo by Debra Kasson-Jones)

2013 photo of the author at the Salt Spring Hills picnic area

Cover photo: Ibex Springs

About the Author

Robert is President of the Kennesaw Historical Society, and Director of Programs and Education for the Kennesaw Museum Foundation. He is also an at-large board member for the Civil War Round Table of Cobb County. He has written several books on Civil War and railroad themes, including:

- *Battle of Allatoona Pass: The Forgotten Battle of Sherman's Atlanta Campaign, The*
- *Battle of Chickamauga: A Brief History, The*
- *Bleeding Kansas: The Real Start of the Civil War*
- *Civil War Prison Camps: A Brief History*
- *Confederate Invasion of New Mexico, The*
- *Famous Songs of the Civil War*
- *Fifteen Most Critical Moments of the Civil War, The*
- *Images of America: Kennesaw*
- *Pennsylvania Railroad: An Illustrated Timeline, The*
- *Reading Railroad: An Illustrated Timeline, The*
- *Retracing the Route of Sherman's Atlanta Campaign and March to the Sea*
- *Ten Best – and Worst – Generals of the Civil War, The*
- *The Battle of Griswoldville: An Infantry Battle on Sherman's March to the Sea*
- *Top 20 Civil War Spies and Secret Agents, The*
- *Top 20 Railroad Songs of All Time, The*
- *Top 25 Most Influential Women of the Civil War, The*
- *W&A, the General, and the Andrews Raid: A Brief History, The*

Robert C. Jones is an ordained elder in the Presbyterian Church. He has written and taught numerous adult Sunday School courses. He is also the author of:

- *25 Most Influential Protestant Leaders in England, The*
- *25 Most Influential Protestant Leaders in the United States, The*
- *25 Most Important Events in the Post-Apostolic Christian Church, The*
- *25 Most Influential Books in the Post-Apostolic Christian Church, The*
- *25 Most Influential People in the Post-Apostolic Christian Church, The*
- *25 People Who Most Influenced the Music of Christianity, The*
- *A Brief History of Protestantism in the United States*

- *A Brief History of the Sacraments: Baptism and Communion*
- *Crusades and the Inquisition: A Brief History, The*
- *Heaven and Hell: In the Bible, the Apocrypha and the Dead Sea Scrolls*
- *Meet the Apostles: Biblical and Legendary Accounts*
- *Monks and Monasteries: A Brief History*
- *Origins of the New Testament, The*
- *Revelation: Background and Commentary*
- *Top 25 Misconceptions About Christianity, The*

Robert has also written several books on "Old West" themes, including:

- *Death Valley Ghost Towns – As They Appear Today*
- *Ghost Towns of Southern Arizona and New Mexico*
- *Ghost Towns of the Mojave National Preserve*
- *Ghost Towns of Western Nevada*
- *Top 10 Gunslingers and Lawmen of the Old West, The*

In 2005, Robert co-authored a business-oriented book entitled *Working Virtually: The Challenges of Virtual Teams*.

In 2013, Robert published *The Leo Beuerman Story: As Told by his Family*.

http://www.rcjbooks.com/
jone442@bellsouth.net

Printed in Great Britain
by Amazon